1iStock.com/Inna Polekhina

THE TROPICAL HOUSEPLANT DOCTOR

AN EXPERT GARDENING GUIDE TO
NURSE SICK & DYING PLANTS
BACK TO VIBRANT HEALTH

RHEA SPENCER

"My green thumb came only as a result of the mistakes I made while learning to see things from the plant's point of view."
— H. Fred Dale

© Copyright 2023 Rhea Spencer. All rights reserved.

The content contained within this book may not be reproduced, duplicated, or transmitted without direct written permission from the author or the publisher.

Under no circumstances will any blame or legal responsibility be held against the publisher or author for any damages, reparation, or monetary loss due to the information contained within this book, either directly or indirectly.

Legal Notice:

This book is copyright protected. It is only for personal use. You cannot amend, distribute, sell, use, quote or paraphrase any part, or the content within this book, without the consent of the author or publisher.

Disclaimer Notice:

Please note the information contained within this document is for educational and entertainment purposes only. All effort has been executed to present accurate, uptodate, reliable, complete information. No warranties of any kind are declared or implied. Readers acknowledge that the author is not engaged in the rendering of legal, financial, medical, or professional advice. The content within this book has been derived from various sources. Please consult a licensed professional before attempting any techniques outlined in this book.

By reading this document, the reader agrees that under no circumstances is the author responsible for any losses, direct or indirect, that are incurred as a result of the use of the information contained within this document, including, but not limited to, errors, omissions, or inaccuracies.

TABLE OF CONTENTS

PREFACE

Dear Reader,

Welcome to the enchanting world of *The Tropical Houseplant Doctor*, a book that will transform your green thumb into a magical wand capable of breathing life and vitality into your beloved leafy companions. I am thrilled you chose to embark on this botanical adventure with me. I assure you that within these pages, you will uncover secrets to revolutionize how you care for your houseplants.

I implore you to resist the temptation of jumping ahead to the commonly known and general facts on a particular houseplant. Now, you may wonder why. The answer lies within the first three chapters of this book. In these chapters, you will encounter a treasure trove of unique antidotes, creative solutions, and myth-breaking advice that will elevate your plant-nurturing skills to unprecedented heights. These chapters hold the essence of *The Tropical Houseplant Doctor*'s methodology, blending the science of horticulture with the intuition of a gardener's heart.

The first three chapters may challenge your preconceived notions and invite you to question the status quo. You will discover that the secret to vibrant foliage lies not in a magic potion or elusive formula but in the nuanced dance of balance. *The Tropical Houseplant Doctor* will empower you to embrace your intuition and trust your instincts, defying the limitations of rigid guidelines.

As you delve into these pages, prepare yourself for an extraordinary journey that transcends the boundaries of conventional horticulture. You will be transported into a realm where plants become sentient beings, silently communicating their needs and desires. Together, we shall decipher their messages and heal them with a touch of tender care and understanding.

Through the lens of *The Tropical Houseplant Doctor*, you will explore the intricate symbiotic relationship between plants and their environment. You will learn how the gentle airflow, the filtered sunlight, and the serene hum of nature's symphony shape the well-being of your leafy companions within the sanctuary of your home. Embrace this understanding, and you will become a medical specialist, skillfully diagnosing and treating the ailments of your cherished plants, creating a healing and harmonious ecosystem indoors.

Before I conclude this preface, I want to express my deepest gratitude to my family for their unwavering support throughout this incredible journey. To my grandmother, whose gift of my first houseplant sparked the seed of curiosity and nurtured my love for the botanical world, I am forever grateful. And to my mother, who graciously provided me with the space to cultivate my passion, allowing my knowledge to bloom alongside the plants that adorned our home.

To all the plant enthusiasts, nature lovers, and curious souls who have paved the way for this book to come to life, thank you for your unwavering enthusiasm and support. Your collective spirit continues to inspire and fuel the pursuit of knowledge and understanding in the realm of plant care.

Now, dear reader, I beseech you to embark on this extraordinary journey through the pages of *The Tropical Houseplant Doctor*. Embrace the art and science of plant care, and in return, witness your houseplants flourish and thrive like never before.

May this book be your guide, your confidant, and your source of inspiration as you begin this botanical adventure. Together, let us unlock the mysteries of the plant kingdom and breathe life into every corner of our homes.

With heartfelt gratitude and green-fingered excitement,
Rhea Spencer

INTRODUCTION

Raising indoor plants is more complex than buying a plant at the nursery and placing it in a pot inside your home. Plants are a hobby and a form of therapy. A domestic environment full of plants looks and feels more pleasant, and tending to those plants can do wonders for your mind. However, plants are not mere objects of decoration— they are living beings that need care and nurturing to develop correctly.

Keeping indoor plants requires you to know each species' needs and particularities. It also requires you to understand your home. A room with windows facing south will be better suited for certain plants than for others. If you have lived in the same place for some time, you may already know everything about that place. Still, when you start to grow your plants, you will view your home with a new perspective.

There are plenty of mistakes one can make while cultivating houseplants indoors. The lack of sunlight is one of the most significant issues since different plants require different types and amounts of light. It is more complex than offering them all the light available, too, for that could dry and burn the leaves, harming your plant.

The humidity of your home and the amount and quality of water you give to your tropical plants is another tricky subject explored in more detail later. Plants are beautiful in the home. Pruning their dead and yellowing leaves helps maintain their aesthetic. Pruning also means pinching the growing tips to form the plant into a desired shape. It may feel like you are harming the plant, but this standard practice improves its health.

Even someone experienced in growing plants outdoors can make mistakes with indoor plants. Whether you are an experienced outdoor grower, indoor plants are already a part of your home life, or you are starting from scratch, this book will offer more than a general overview of how to nurture your collection. You'll find unique, in-depth, precise houseplant information in one book.

Growing indoor plants is a fulfilling and fascinating activity that can boost your mental health and relieve stress if done correctly. Nevertheless, it can cause anxiety if you do not know enough to be successful. With all the activity of modern life, you cannot expect to offer your full attention to your plants. Here you will find advice and techniques to save time and give you peace of mind when you are not home.

Looking at a once-beautiful plant and seeing only decaying leaves is depressing. That sight is sad enough to keep many from wanting to grow houseplants again. You don't have to give up, but educating yourself before taking another go at it is a good idea. This way, you will learn time-tested techniques in plant care, change your perspective with informed insight, and even experience that "aha" moment when you know you understand enough to have an excellent chance of success.

There's plenty of information online about growing your houseplants, but here you have a comprehensive guide with the essential facts you need to understand about houseplants. In this book, you will learn from my experience, as I have been learning about plants for decades and continue to teach and learn on this topic. Taking on a new type of houseplant is exciting; an educated eye can adapt unique circumstances to the plant's needs and help any plant thrive.

Nature fascinates me, and I think of myself as a steward of unwavering love for Mother Nature and the Earth. I acquired this love during my early years in rural New Jersey and brought it to my current home of forty years in Central Texas. From a very young age, science has resonated with me. I studied for over eight years across two universities to major in biology and chemistry. My analytical mind loves to ask why, where, what if, and how. My patience and growing knowledge base led me to many unique solutions to common houseplant problems. These explanations, methods, and solutions to problems are unique, time tested, and you will find them here in this book.

Academic jargon ruled the day for much of my university life. I have tried to break down the terminology and the mystery of plants into simple, accessible language so that the lightbulb will go off in your head and you will "get it."

Saving a buck and being frugal are other college memories that prompted me to print in black and white. Black and white images in the paperback version lower the printing costs and gives savings back to you. Access the striking images in full color for free by typing the following link into your browser.

https://docs.google.com/document/d/1xwYRnKu_dQ9BKDcyhag1J17xEHi5E-Gr20uH5g9DHvek/edit?usp=sharing

Later, we'll go through the most popular houseplants and translate all the fundamental aspects of raising them into simple, fun steps. Combining my experience with my academic education, I will teach you what you need to know to succeed in this fascinating hobby.

Let's get started.

6istock.com/Ralf Geithe

CHAPTER 1:

PLANT POWER

EXPLORING THE WONDERS OF THE PLANT KINGDOM

As living and thinking creatures, we have instincts that help us to stay alive. Through those instincts, we know we need food, water, warmth, and sleep. Plants undergo a similar process, anticipating the necessary resources to help them stay alive. To see your plants thrive, you need to learn their needs in depth.

The first association we tend to make with a person is their name. It helps us connect, identify, and talk about them to others. Learning the names of plants is just as important when you want to gather the best care tips. It helps develop a relationship with the plants we care for and to learn more about them.

When you go to the nursery, you won't ask for a Dracaena sanderiana but for lucky bamboo. Why then learn these names? You will see that plants closely related in their scientific classification will thrive under similar conditions. If you were successful with a plant from a particular family or genus, the likelihood is high that you will get similar results with a related plant.

THE WONDERFUL WORLD OF PLANTS

All living things are classified into kingdoms: animals, protozoa, fungi—and, of course, plants.

The scientific classification system is divided into the categories below, from the broadest to the most specific:

- **Kingdom**
- **Phylum**
- **Class**
- **Order**
- **Family**
- **Genus**
- **Species**

Plant phyla are separated into categories like flowering plants, ferns, and mosses. Most houseplants are angiosperms or flowering plants (although not all will bloom indoors, as most are appreciated for their leaves instead).

Down the classification funnel, a plant's nomenclature splits into genus and species. The genus is the first part of the name, and members of a genus are like cousins to each other, meaning they often thrive with similar environments and care requirements. (This knowledge will help when selecting new additions to your houseplant collection.) The species, the second part of the name, hones in on the individual plant and its particular characteristics, like siblings. Most houseplants are recognizable by their genus and species name, which combine to form their botanical names.

Let's use an orchid as an example:

Group: Angiosperm
Family: Orchidaceae
Genus: Dendrobium
Species: *victoriae-reginae*
Botanical name: *Dendrobium victoriae-reginae*
Common name: Queen Victoria's orchid

The species' name defines specific aspects of the plant, such as the shape of the plant, its color, the shape of its leaves, or who discovered it. Houseplants are regionally referred to by popular common names or nicknames derived from their botanical names. Examples include the goldfish plant, whose flowers resemble this popular pet, the airplane or spider plant with its dangling babies, and the fiddle leaf fig with leaves resembling the instrument.

THE BASIC PLANT STRUCTURE

Almost all plants are autotrophs, meaning they use photosynthesis to produce food. (The only plants not autotrophs are parasitic plants, which cannot photosynthesize and must gain nutrition from their host plant instead.) The process of photosynthesis combines sunlight, water, carbon dioxide, and minerals taken from the soil, which together produce the nutrients the plant needs.

A plant organism includes roots, stems, leaves, and reproductive organs (flowers, cones, spores, etc.). All plants, except mosses and liverworts, are vascular, transporting nutrients in water through an internal tubular structure.

Roots

There are many different types of root system designs; plant families tend to have similar root systems. The metabolic requirements of the plant and its environment dictate the root system needed to meet the needs of the plant body. In plants, this underground organ secures and supports the plant, receiving the water and nutrients needed for photosynthesis.

Roots have a cap at their tips, which senses gravity and protects them as they grow through the soil. Above that cap, there's a zone of cell division, or meristem, which makes that growth possible. Above the meristem, we find the zone of elongation, where there's rapid cell growth to push the root deeper, and finally, the zone of differentiation, which develops plant tissue, including vascular components, for use throughout the plant.

Next, we find the root hairs and the root crown or collar. Root hairs increase the area for roots to get water and exchange gases (oxygen and carbon dioxide) and nutrients with the soil mixture. The root crown often resides above the soil line and is where the roots emerge from the stem.

Water enters the roots through diffusion. Diffusion is the process by which water moves from an area of high concentration to an area of low concentration. A way to visualize diffusion is to place a drop of food coloring into a container of clear water. With no assistance, the dye diffuses from the area of high concentration (the drop where it entered the container) and eventually evenly colors the rest of the clear water. When the dye is wholly diffused, the concentration level of the dye in the water is the same or at equilibrium throughout the vessel.

When watering houseplants, think of the water added as the dye and the inside of the roots as the transparent area. A plant's root cell walls are semi-permeable to water. This characteristic allows water to diffuse freely into the roots until the roots become saturated. No more water can enter the roots at saturation because the water gradient across the root barrier has equalized. Job done. Something else has to happen for more water to diffuse into the roots. The water needs to get used up so the space inside the roots will be drier than outside their cell walls. (All this will tie together in the photosynthesis section.)

It is crucial to know that plants cannot absorb water at will. Although diffusion and absorption may appear similar, they are entirely different processes. When potted houseplants receive more water than they can handle, the water sits there and stagnates, keeping the air from entering the soil. Within this anaerobic (without air) environment, decay sets in.

Roots function at their best under aerobic conditions, which means in the presence of oxygenated air. When a plant is continuously exposed to excessive moisture, the oxygen gets pushed from the soil, the soil compacts, and creates an anaerobic environment ideal for decay. Roots need oxygen for metabolic reasons essential for optimal health and function. Roots can be thought of as the lungs of the plant. Perhaps you have heard the rule do not overwater your houseplants. It is best to let their roots breathe.

Propagation in water, with no soil present, enables roots to flourish in an oxygen-rich environment with dissolved nutrients. No soil is present, nor are the pathogens and fungal components that produce decay. Roots have an easier, simplified life growing in water. Keep in mind not all species are suitable for life without soil.

When the tips of the roots start to poke out of the pot's drainage holes or roots start becoming obvious at the top of the soil, it's an indicator that you need to move the houseplant to a larger planter.

Stems

Nutrients and water are transported through the stems to the leaves by way of veins, to make photosynthesis possible. The veins that bring water and minerals from the root to the leaf are called xylem. The ones that transport those nutrients to other parts of the plant are called phloem. This scenario is analogous to the mammalian artery and vein system, although plants do not have a pumping heart.

Vascular plants have nodes and internodes in their stems from which leaves, branches, flowers, and fruits emerge. Roots form from nodes when propagating.

Stems are the backbone of the plant, offering it a structure to support branches, leaves and vascular components. Some green stems can perform photosynthesis, food storage, vegetative propagation, and even asexual reproduction.

Leaves

Leaves are mainly responsible for photosynthesis, which we'll discuss later. Here, we are going to focus on the leaf structure, which includes:

- **Waxy cuticle**: As the name implies, the waxy cuticle is a thin layer of waxy-like material that covers the leaf surface. It's produced by the plant to keep it from losing water, protect it from heat, and protect the photosynthetic cells that make the plant's food.
- **Blade, petiole, veins**: The blade, which is commonly known as the leaf, is the green surface responsible for photosynthesis. It connects to the main stem by a smaller stem called the petiole. The visible vascular structures of the blade are called veins.

- **Hairs or trichomes**: Leaf hairs, or trichomes, are long filaments—similar to body hair—present on leaves and stems. They control the loss of humidity and airflow around the plant and create an atmosphere under the leaves.
- **Stomata**: Stomata are tiny openings or pores on the underside of the leaves. These pores allow gas exchange between the leaves and the air. They regulate carbon dioxide (CO_2), oxygen (O_2), and water vapor (H_2O). They have small guard cells resembling lips that open and close the pore to enable this exchange. Gases and water vapor can enter and exit the stomata.

Some plants are more famous for their dark foliage than their flowers. Large flat leaves can take lower light conditions since they have a larger surface to collect light from, indicating that a plant can survive in low light and without direct sun. Fleshy leaves hold more water and are prone to sunburning. Sunburning happens when sunbeams strike the leaf and melt through the waxy cuticle. Prolonged exposure to direct sun heats up the water inside the leaves enough to destroy the leaf tissue. Small leaves can take more direct light for longer hours, allow for more air movement and endure drier conditions.

Flowers
Flowers work as the main reproductive organ in most plants. They have male and female organs and produce ovules, which are fertilized and develop into seeds.

Seeds
Seeds nourish and protect embryos and sprouting plants. They serve as a food reserve for the young plant to use while developing. Each seed has its particular characteristics, which will generate plants of different sizes and shapes. They are, in large part, responsible for the propagation of a plant species.

Although they do not amble around, the idea that a plant functions in an analogous way to people and animals may be dawning on you. Plants get classified with proper names and nicknames. Stems act as a spine for the plant and can bleed out fluids when cut. Hairs protect the immediate environment in their personal space. Plants breathe in and out through openings (stomata) with lip-like cells as regulators (guard cells) together with lung-like structures (roots) underground. Sap, water and nutrients flow between these organs in structures known as veins. Plants exhibit abilities to reproduce through sex organs identified as gender specific. There is documentation that plants respond to sounds. The next section reveals more similarities and differences.

THE PROCESS OF PHOTOSYNTHESIS

People and animals eliminate waste daily. It is a chore to clean up. Plants, on the other hand, make no visible waste. Not only are they clean to have around, but they also purify the air.

Plants' ability to enact the chemical process of turning light energy, carbon dioxide, water, and minerals into oxygen and sugars—known as photosynthesis—is responsible for life on Earth. All plants (except parasitic and mutated plants) can photosynthesize; they stay healthy and thrive through this process.

The two processes of photosynthesis are the light reactions, where the plant harvests sunlight to make oxygen and energy, and the dark reactions, where the plant uses energy from the light reactions to produce carbon dioxide and sugars, which fuel its growth. Both reactions happen simultaneously in the leaf while the plant gets light energy.

A chlorophyll pigment inside the plant's leaf cells is responsible for the light reactions. Chlorophyll absorbs red and blue light waves and reflects green light waves, giving plants their green appearance. Plants will not benefit from green light, as they cannot absorb it, which is why many grow lights come in shades of red and blue: these are the colors the plant needs to fuel photosynthesis.

The dark reactions of photosynthesis need water to occur. Water moves into the roots through diffusion and is released from the leaves into the atmosphere through transpiration. Transpiration refers to the evaporation of water at the stomata on the undersides of the leaves. By exquisite design, a negative pressure, or vacuum, exists within vascular plants, pulling the water up from the roots to exit the stomata on the underside of the leaves. (This negative pressure phenomenon exists in human veins as well.)

Photosynthesis, in conjunction with transpiration, is the "something else" needed for the water in the roots to get used up by moving through the plant and exiting the stomata.

On a chemistry level, when a plant receives both water and light, the light photons become excited and split a water molecule (H_2O) to produce oxygen and hydrogen molecules. The hydrogen molecules combine with other molecular compounds containing nitrogen and phosphorus (N and P, which are crucial elements of most fertilizers for this reason). The resulting biochemical reactions—the aforementioned dark reactions—create sugars the plant uses for energy. Meanwhile, the oxygen within water is a waste product to the plant and escapes through the leaves' stomata as a byproduct of transpiration and photosynthesis.

Thus, photosynthesis feeds the plant and provides it with all the energy it needs to grow, maintain its structure, and perform other necessary functions. Moreover, photosynthesis sustains human and animal life on Earth. Whereas animal respiration works by inhaling oxygen and exhaling carbon dioxide as an end product, plants use photosynthesis to convert carbon dioxide and water into the oxygen we breathe. Animal respiration is both the inverse of photosynthesis and its complement.

Plants are vital to our survival—and we can be vital to theirs. Just as we can benefit from the oxygen and air purification that houseplants provide to us, they can benefit from the care and understanding we give them.

One other note: variegated and albino houseplants have genetic mutations where the chlorophyll pigmentation within their leaves is partially or entirely absent. This lack of pigmentation leads to white or cream patterns on the leaves. An all-white leaf cannot photosynthesize, and a half-white leaf will require more light than a solid green one. Variegated houseplants are highly coveted because of their striking colors, patterns, and extreme rarity within nature. A variegated leaf might revert to a more solid green appearance in low-light conditions.

HOW TO PROVIDE PLANTS WITH WHAT THEY NEED

In the wild, plants tend to grow in an environment offering the conditions to thrive. When bringing these plants into the home environment, recreate conducive conditions for the plant to develop and survive. Relax with the understanding that houseplants tolerate a range of light, water, temperature, and humidity. What is comfortable for you and your family will accommodate a variety of houseplants.

Put that flexibility into perspective using a balance scale analogy. Consider the growth requirements between the same plant in low light versus bright light conditions. Generally, in low light, photosynthesis happens more slowly. Therefore, water usage slows down. Longer periods can go by between thorough drenching. (Watering less with smaller quantities of water will not be effective and is detrimental.)

The same plant in brighter light photosynthesizes faster. It needs thorough watering more often. The "in general" guidance does not encompass atmospheric humidity, soil composition combined with fertilization, or room temperature, which can play into the balance of photosynthesis and watering needs. But this general play between available light and watering needs guides us in houseplant care through the seasons.

Light

Like most organisms, plant life depends on the sun's energy. That does not mean that all plants can tolerate direct sunlight for most of the time, if at all. Finding a place to access enough natural light may be challenging. Ideally, the sun streaming into your home accommodates various tropical houseplants. If not, artificial light is an option.

Look for 4 to 6 hours daily of the prescribed best natural light. If needed, supplement with artificial light between 4 to 8 hours daily. In the absence of the ideal natural light, ten to twelve hours a day of artificial light works well for non-flowering specimens. Use a timer with your lights for regularity.

Sunlight

Sunlight from the east, or morning light, gives a few daily hours of direct brightness and tends towards a mellow ambiance for the rest of the day.

By late mid-morning, southern exposure sunlight ramps up (following eastern light) and lasts most of the day. Here is the most intense, brightest and hottest direct sunlight. Plants can live successfully by placing them closer or farther away from this light source.

As it moves into the west, the sun shines hot and bright for a while longer before calming down into the sunset. Be mindful of which plants get this exposure, since intensity can be bright and hot for an hour or two, with overall brightness most of the day.

Northern light tends to be mellow, diffused, and ambient, with little opportunity for bright, direct rays. At best, this location offers indirect light, but only briefly. Most of the day in northern exposure offers evenly diffused low light, sufficient for photosynthesis.

It is essential to familiarize ourselves with other types of light that impact houseplants and often get mentioned in care instructions, such as bright, indirect, and low light.

Bright direct light comes through the window with no obstruction, including drapes or blinds, casting a clear, sharp shadow when you hold your hand 1 foot over a piece of paper. Bright indirect light exists just outside the direct sunbeam area.

Filtered or indirect light, also known as moderate light, comes through a curtain or from a distant window. It casts a fuzzy but distinct shadow, following the same previous method.

Shade, or ambient light, lacks sunlight or artificial light. Shade-tolerant plants thrive in this low light, especially with higher humidity levels.

There are four main types of artificial light available for plant growth: incandescent lighting, fluorescent light, light-emitting diodes, and high-intensity light. (Lighting et al.).

Incandescent Bulbs

With an abundance of red light and a small amount of blue light, incandescent bulbs are not the most effective sole source of light for plants. The heat they generate can harm plants and remove moisture from the air. Keep these at a safe distance from the leaves.

Their main appeal is that they are a cheap option and are present in most modern homes. It is best to use incandescent bulbs in conjunction with other sources of light.

Fluorescent Tubes

An affordable and efficient source of light for indoor plants, fluorescent tubes are one of the most popular options. They are available in different designs that emit little heat. The output of the fluorescent tubes, designed for plant growth, is balanced by higher production in the blue and red spectrum, and will also tout full spectrum or grow light labeling. Screw-in fluorescent grow lights are now available to fit the same socket as incandescent bulbs.

Light-Emitting Diodes (LEDs)

Popularly known as LED lights, light-emitting diodes can be programmed to emit different levels of blue and red lights and to imitate the color temperature of sunlight. They consume little energy and have a long lifespan, which makes them a good investment.

Spotlights

Most spotlights are incandescent and ineffective as grow lights. Spotlights are not the best option since they have an unbalanced mix of red and blue light, but they can provide extra light if necessary. Spotlights can run hot and sap moisture from the environment, so do not burn the plants with poor placement.

Water Quality and Humidity

Different plants have different watering needs, which include the amount and frequency of watering and the humidity in the air. It is essential to know those individual needs to protect the plant's life cycle from ruin.

Overwatering can be deadly to many species, especially cacti and succulents. Underwatering also harms plants with disastrous results. Both are discussed in chapter two of this book.

Water quality needs solid consideration for the growth and health of houseplants.

Water high in salts and other minerals (especially hard water) can accumulate in the potting medium over time, creating a build-up of harmful salts and minerals that can inhibit plant growth and health. Plan on repotting yearly if this is your case, as flushing helps clear some but not all salts.

Some chemicals in the water can be harmful to houseplants and affect their health. Free water testing is available to find out what is in your water.

Some of the common chemicals that can be detrimental to houseplants are:

1. **Chlorine and chloramines:** Chlorine and chloramines are added to tap water to disinfect it, but it can be toxic to plants causing yellowing leaves and stunted growth.
2. **Fluoride:** Fluoride can accumulate in plant tissues and cause leaf necrosis, stunted growth, and reduced flower production.
3. **Sodium:** High levels of sodium in water can interfere with a plant's ability to absorb essential nutrients, leading to stunted growth and yellowing leaves.
4. **Calcium and magnesium:** While calcium and magnesium are essential micronutrients for plants, excess levels of these ions in water can cause buildup in the soil, leading to soil imbalances and reduced plant growth.
5. **Heavy metals:** Heavy metals such as lead, copper, and zinc can accumulate in plant tissues and cause toxicity symptoms, including stunted growth, yellowing leaves, and reduced flowering.

Therefore, using clean, chemical-free water for watering indoor plants is advisable. There are a number of sources for good water for houseplants.

Obviously, turn to the tap. Just make sure to let tap water sit out for 24 hours before use to allow the chlorine to dissipate. Chloramines and other heavy metals in tap water will not dissipate into the air. The most economical fix to removing these persistent chemicals is available by adding a water conditioner to the plants water. Inexpensive and sold to treat tap water for fish tanks, water conditioners eliminate chlorine, chloramines, heavy metals, and ammonia.

Use fish tank water to water houseplants when available. The conditioned state of the water and added nutrients from the fish are a treat for your plants.

Rainwater can benefit houseplants, as it is naturally pH neutral to slightly acidic and contains some essential minerals and nutrients. The nature of rainwater aids in nutrient availability in the soil.

In some cases, distilled or purified water may be used. Filtered water is best.

Humidity, or air moisture, is another factor that can affect a plant's health—some plants, identified by their thick and waxy leaves or documented fussy nature, like humidity more than others. Using a small indoor humidifier near a grouping of plants requiring extra moisture can often solve a dry air problem.

Another option is to move plants to different parts of the house or office according to their needs. The bathroom and the kitchen are the most convenient places to keep plants that love moisture. Consider the lighting situation when choosing high humidity-loving plants for these areas.

One helpful technique to increase air moisture is to group houseplants in the same environment so that they will increase the humidity by themselves. Taking this idea to the next level, one could use a humidity tray to determine which plants get a higher humidity level.

To make a DIY humidity tray at home, place some pebbles or river stones on a waterproof tray and pour on enough water to cover the rocks. Place the plants on top and ensure the water does not seep into the pot's drainage hole.

Commercial humidity trays are made of long-lasting plastic with high sides. Instead of pebbles as the base, inside lies a synthetic fabric called a wicking mat. The mats distribute the water evenly. Clay pots absorb any water they touch, so the humidity tray could be a great option for keeping plants in terra cotta watered while on vacation, in addition to adding humidity to plants in ceramic cache pots.

Ensure humidity-loving plants are not around drafty doors, uninsulated windows, or blowing air from conditioning and heating ducts.

Misting might raise the humidity for a short period, but it mostly gets the leaves wet and makes little change to the atmosphere. Properly-misted plants should look like a delicate dew has fallen on them. Some plants can live under constant misting, while others endure it once or twice weekly. Others, like succulents, do not like misting at all. I do not use misting sprays to increase humidity and only use this technique to wash my plants' leaves. Many plant parents use misters, and there is little harm in the practice.

Plants can also benefit from a gentle shower once or twice a year. Bring them outside or into the bathroom, and wash their leaves with a gentle tepid spray to eliminate dust, dirt, and clinging insects.

Nutrients

Plants need proper nutrition to function and grow correctly. Even though each plant has different needs, commercially available houseplant fertilizers fit the needs of a wide variety of houseplants. Dilutions come in handy when there is uncertainty around the houseplant's ability to handle a full-strength dose (in cases of plant rescue and newly planted propagations). Increase the normal recommended amount of water to create a diluted strength as needed.

The primary essential nutrients needed for optimal growth of any plant that photosynthesizes are nitrogen (N), phosphorus (P), and potassium (K), commonly referred to as NPK.

Nitrogen

Nitrogen is an essential plant nutrient, supporting many functions and processes. It is also a key chlorophyll component, allowing plants to perform photosynthesis and produce energy.

Nitrogen supports the growth and development of leaves, stems, and branches and helps synthesize amino acids, nucleic acids, and other essential plant compounds. It also helps to improve the overall health and vigor of the plant, leading to more robust green growth and increasing resistance to stress and diseases.

Phosphorus

Phosphorus is essential for plants. It is involved in energy transfer and storage and in the growth and development of roots, stems, flowers, and fruit. Plants also require phosphorous to form DNA, RNA, and ATP, which are all crucial components of the plant's genetic material and energy storage.

Potassium

Potassium, the third essential element, regulates water balance and produces sugars and starches. It is involved in several key processes in a plant's organs, including stomatal regulation, water balance, stress tolerance, protein synthesis, photosynthesis, and finally, fruit and seed production.

Fertilizers are sold with the NPK ratio prominently displayed. The first number represents nitrogen, the second is phosphorus, and the potassium ratio is last. Fertilize your plants regularly with a balanced, water-soluble fertilizer that contains NPK. Balanced means all the numbers and the ratios are the same, such as a 5-5-5. Commercial ratios are sometimes balanced for a particular task. For example, a higher middle number promotes flowers. Therefore, it is balanced for flower production or balanced for fruit trees. Nitrogen promotes healthy leaf growth, so a higher first number will achieve vibrant green coloration. Always read the label. Some houseplants prefer slow-release fertilizers that provide nutrients over a more extended period.

Fish emulsion typically has an NPK (nitrogen, phosphorus, potassium) ratio of 5-2-2, meaning it contains higher levels of nitrogen (5%) compared to phosphorus (2%) and potassium (2%). Fish emulsion is an excellent fertilizer for plants.

In addition to NPK, indoor plants also need secondary nutrients like calcium, magnesium, and sulfur and micronutrients like iron, manganese, and zinc. These lesser nutrients are provided by the potting mix when the potting mix is fresh and well-maintained.

Plants also require a soil pH balance to absorb these nutrients properly. A soil pH that is too acidic or alkaline can limit particular plant's ability to absorb the necessary nutrients, leading to poor growth and health. Know which plants respond to higher acidity or alkalinity. Peat moss, pine needles and used coffee grounds increases acidity. Limestone, wood ash, and crushed oyster shells as soil amendments help with alkalinity.

Hydrogen Peroxide

Hydrogen peroxide (H_2O_2) proves to be an elixir worth using. An amazing tonic for the houseplant, it improves overall health and growth; hydrogen peroxide can disinfect the soil, sterilize gardening tools, and stop the spread of root rot.

It is primarily used as a soil drench to provide oxygen and improve soil aeration. It helps to maintain an aerobic environment for the roots to absorb nutrients and water.

However, adding hydrogen peroxide as a soil drench does not deter bugs and pests. While some applications of hydrogen peroxide can control certain fungal diseases, it is not an effective insecticide.

It is imperative to dilute hydrogen peroxide first. A general guideline is to mix one part 3% hydrogen peroxide with 4 parts water before applying it to the soil. You can disinfect your plant with 1 teaspoon of H_2O_2 diluted in 8 ounces of water. Excess hydrogen peroxide can harm the roots and lead to stress, so don't use it on your plants more than once a month (Russell, n.d.).

As you continue your journey into raising tropical plants indoors, you might feel tempted to acquire new specimens, vases, and other equipment. But the plants you already have in your house are the ideal place to start. These familiar forms will help you learn what success looks like, offer opportunities for experimentation, and teach which mistakes to avoid.

The time will come to buy new houseplants, which we will discuss in the next chapter. I will teach you how to shop for the best houseplants so that your joy and accomplishment will continue once you get them home and nestle them in.

CHAPTER 2:
SETTLING IN

TRANSITIONING YOUR HOUSEPLANTS TO THEIR NEW DIGS

Nurseries are magical places where plants grow and develop their personalities. Large nursery operations ship and deliver houseplants to local area big box stores. Shopping at a local nursery center never gets old. There is something new each week.

But plants are available in all types of stores nowadays, and a simple visit to the market or the mall could lead to discovering a gorgeous new addition for your plant family. Found online, many independents and large enterprises have plant facilities that ship through the mail. Keeping an open mind and eye for buying opportunities in unexpected places can prove rewarding.

Finding the right plant to bring home to nurture is a unique feeling. Many factors can influence that choice, such as the size of your home, how much sunlight comes in through the windows, your time constraints, and the presence of pets and children. When you have a few plants doing exceptionally well and there is more room on their table, shelf, or floor, it doesn't get any better than finding a houseplant that fits right in.

Where Should Your New Baby Live?

The level of light is crucial when taking care of plants. Your living room may only see sunlight for less than 2 hours daily. A grow light can be a good solution in that case. Alternatively, you might have constant access to intense sunlight. Is there a place one to ten feet away from the sun's direct rays for the plant to live? Can sheer curtains or directional blinds mitigate the intense light? Most houseplants need 6-8 daily hours of some degree of indirect light, whether bright or muted, and can scorch if left in direct southern or western sunlight for too long.

Each plant has its peculiarities, punctuated by the balance of water, light, and soil conditions. Some houseplants need constant love and care and will die if you don't tend to them promptly. Other houseplants have stronger constitutions and will survive your oversight along the way. Ask yourself if you're methodic and disciplined enough to handle the more delicate species, and always be honest with yourself.

Despite all that, I still defend that any person can raise houseplants. The trick is to manage your limitations, understand your environment, and know your plant's requirements rather than denying them.

6 TIPS FOR BUYING THE BEST PLANTS

Here is some helpful information. Take these tips into consideration when you're adding a new plant to your collection.

Start Smaller

Contemplate beginning with smaller houseplants in pots sized at 2-, 3-, or 4-inches instead of spending big money on larger plants. Not all plants grow easily indoors; you must experiment before finding the ones that suit your environment. Once familiar with the challenges, you can confidently invest significant funds in bigger plants. Purchasing a large plant that disagrees with your home and spirals into a miserable state can prove an expensive lesson in houseplant care. It is all right to immediately transplant the little plants from 2 and 3-inch pots into 4-inch pots. If you don't, you will go in circles watering since tiny pots dry out quickly.

Shop Local if Possible

Find a local nursery that you can trust and where you will receive personalized treatment. A good nursery will have specialized employees who can give you precious advice about what you're buying and how to care for it.

Big retailers give their plants less love and care than a local nursery and the employees might not know much about the selections. If you are buying in a big store, take extra time to pick the right plants. The selection is usually fantastic! Closeouts and discounts are often reserved for less healthy, neglected specimens. The prettier ones are often the healthiest but are also more expensive.

When shopping online, ask if care requirements and instructions come with the plant.

Ask About Returns

Check for warranties and guarantees locally and when ordering online. Shipping and carrier issues could delay delivery, and rough handling may cause delicate plants to arrive damaged or overly stressed. Consider the time of year the order is placed since extreme heat and cold can harm a box of plants. Try to place online orders in the spring or fall when ambient temperatures are conducive to safe travel. For added consumer protection, document the state of the plant's arrival with pictures.

Check the Information on the Pot

Check that an informational name tag comes with the plant. Look for the plant's name, recommended light and water conditions, ideal soil and pH requirements, fertilizer schedule, and humidity needs.

Wait to throw away this tag or sticker. It has precious information you can use while raising the plant. Keep that information until you've memorized it. If the tag or sticker is missing, explore additional resources for the necessary information.

Check for Healthy Foliage, Absence of Pests, and Ample Potting Medium

The plant tag can only inform you so much, and you need to analyze the plant's foliage and sometimes the roots to determine its health. Look for robust growth, emerging leaves, and firm strength in the stems. A few dead leaves aren't bad, but buying a plant with clear signs of rot, yellowing, limpness, or pests will give you an unnecessary headache. Look for signs of pests and cobwebs, which indicate the plant can quickly become unhealthy. Pests can leave spots, discolorations, or minor bite marks on the leaves and stem.

The soil level should be near the top of the planter, offering a clear picture of what type of potting mix is used. White mold should not be present. White mold could mean the plant stayed moist constantly, resulting in rotten roots. Please don't be shy about asking an attendant if you can check the roots. When permission is granted, gently attempt to lift the houseplant out of its pot to check for root-bound status.

If soil is going to fall out all over the place, stop. In this case, the roots are usually good. If the plant slides easily from the pot because it is rootbound with little soil present, continue to take the opportunity to look at the root structure. If it's not grossly rootbound and some potting mix is visible, carry on with the acquisition, but only if you still want to get it and have the means to repot into a larger planter soon.

There is a disturbing trend employed at some nurseries that deserves mentioning. Plants, and their 2-, 3-, or 4-inch plastic starter pots are quickly transferred into a larger 6-inch pot, and camouflaged with potting mix before shipment. The 6-inch potted plant is purchased, only to find that the roots are strangling themselves inside a smaller starter pot. The detrimental repotting practice also presents itself with mesh fabric and spray-on polystyrene foam instead of tiny plastic pots.

Philodendrons, Scindapsus, and Monstera varieties reveal this terrible trend more than other houseplants. Buyer beware, and check for this troubling practice by removing the plant, gently squeezing the root ball, and checking for embedded plastic, mesh, or hard foam. Or, once at home, gingerly push the blunt end of a wooden skewer almost halfway through the root ball to check for a smaller plastic pot, being careful not to skewer any roots.

Quarantine New Plants

Always quarantine a new plant for a few days to a week to make sure no pests tagged along in the soil or on the plant itself. Get out a bright light and a magnifying glass, if needed, to inspect the crevices thoroughly before placing the houseplant in your home. Even if you trust where you bought the plant, this is a crucial step to avoid introducing diseases and infecting the rest of your plants. Consider spraying the top of the soil and the plant with neem oil as a preventative.

TYPES OF PLANTERS

Choosing the right container for your plant is vital. You must take the plant's needs into account, but also the space that you have and what will fit in it.

A beautiful tropical houseplant in a pretty planter ticks the box and is a pleasure to behold. Planters highlight the more creative aspect of this hobby and allow for the expression of personal taste and creativity. On the other hand, there is nothing wrong with camouflaging a plant's plastic nursery pot by placing it inside a ceramic vessel to catch water runoff (a cache pot).

Design, style, and color matter in a home but must take secondary consideration to the size, shape, and drainage method of a planter. Look for a balance of width to depth. Extra tall and narrow, or large tall pots can harm smaller plants and plants with a shallow root system. Problems may arise when excessive dampness gets held in the soil outside of the root's boundary. Constant dampness can lead to anaerobic conditions, decay and root rot. Understand that the mechanics of the proper planter has as much to do with the success of your houseplant as the light, water, and proper soil composition.

Here are some aspects to look for when selecting planters. The best pots tend to have an easily accessible opening at the top, with sides gently sloping to a flat bottom with drainage holes. The drainage holes are sized well and often there is more than one. These perfectly shaped and designed modern planter choices come in various sizes.

Houseplants started taking the world by storm during the Victorian age. Consequently, vintage ceramic planters with unique footed shapes, animal figurines, unique drip trays, and other delightful oddities are available for potted plants. When there is no drainage hole, use the vessel as a cache pot. Shop thrift stores, garage sales, antique shops, and online for vintage diversity.

Be aware of ceramic planters with a cute little matching drip saucer fused onto the bottom. These drip saucers barely hold any water, offer thin spaces for water to escape, and have a great propensity for clogging. Once dirt or bark pieces get through the drain hole and become trapped between the bottom of the vessel and the fused-on drip saucer, the drainage at the outside edge of the pot stops working. Water stays trapped, allowing for a backlog, poor drainage, and problems.

Many plastic pot designs allow the drip saucer to be removed, but the saucer is also designed to sit very tight and snug to the bottom of the pot. Water gets trapped in this tray unless you tip the planter over on its side for the water to escape. Indeed, this task needs to be done; otherwise, the bottom of the pot will be sitting in water to the detriment of the houseplant. Salts and minerals from the sitting water tend to crust at the edge of these types of drip trays, further exacerbating the drainage issue and detracting from the nice esthetics of the ensemble.

Look for a deep, removable drip tray, or a separate piece that compliments the planter. Fused-on drip saucers, shallow saucers, and drip trays that fit snugly lead to watering issues because the tendency is to use just enough water so that the drip tray does not overflow and make a mess. The saucer must be deep enough to hold the runoff from watering the plant properly while not being inconvenient to use. Otherwise, the worry becomes about watering just enough to satisfy the drip tray's existence and not about the plant's health. Drip trays can be removed altogether in favor of cache pots.

I tend to stay away from planters with an opening smaller than the widest part of the vessel because of problems at transplanting time. Usually, instead of breaking the pot, the plant gets mutilated while trying to get the root ball out. I also tend to avoid planters with an hourglass shape. Invariably, the root ball at the bottom of the pot will not fit through the constricted middle section of the planter.

Here are six of the most popular types of planters. ("7 Best Planter Materials," 2021; Wooden Planters, n.d.):

Cache pots

These overpots or nice-looking vessels do not have drainage holes and are commonly used to disguise plastic nursery pots. A cache pot can be made of any material that holds water; ceramic and plastic are most readily available. Using cache pots is, in fact, highly recommended for various reasons. They make the task of watering less messy by holding the runoff. Cache pots can be placed anywhere in the home with little fear of experiencing water damage to the furniture, floors, or windowsills. Most importantly, cache pots allow the excess water time to reabsorb back into the soil through the main pot's drainage holes, ensuring the planting medium gets proper and total saturation. Bottom watering, allowing the planter to wick up water from the drainage holes, is best done with a cache pot.

When using cache pots, you must empty the excess water that accumulates after 10 to 15 minutes of watering, and don't wait more than a day to empty the runoff. Monitor for signs of overwatering. Use flat stones or pebbles in the bottom of the cache pot to keep the plant's main pot out of the water, if need be. Stick felt dots to the bottom of the cache pots to allow airflow underneath and to prevent watermarks.

Ceramic

Apart from looking excellent in different shapes, colors, and sizes, glazed ceramic planters typically have excellent drainage through the ever-present large hole at the bottom of the vessel. Be wary of fused-on drip trays. Ceramics are also heavier and more expensive, but they tend to last decades.

Clay

Charming, yet delicate, orange or white terracotta clay is more porous than other materials and needs careful handling. It will easily crack, chip, freeze and break. The porous characteristic allows for more air exchange, which prevents root rot. However, it also means that plants will dry out much faster, and you must water them more often and thoroughly. It's advisable to soak terracotta to saturate the clay before potting in them and occasionally once in use. Salts and minerals will collect and also leach out through the sides of the pot over time and make the pot less porous. Plan on cleaning off the salts and minerals yearly. Terra cotta can be painted on the outside to help with moisture retention.

Glass

Terrariums and glass planters are well-suited to humidity-loving plants and look fantastic when displayed as a showpiece. Since the glass keeps the roots from exchanging oxygen with the outside environment, and they don't often come with drainage holes, it's important to use layers of pebbles under a well-draining soil mix so air can circulate. Without drainage or air flow, take care when planting succulents or cacti in these.

Metal

Metal planters are not as common for in-home use, although they are very attractive and worth holding out for. They offer little ventilation and absorb heat quickly, which can stress the plant. Take added care to avoid direct sunbeams.

Plastic

Plastic is the most common and controversial, as it is unsustainably made from non-renewable materials. Aside from that, plastic is an inert substance; it does not react with soil or amendments. It can last decades and works perfectly when the drainage holes are right. (Be wary of the attached drip trays!). There is no airflow through the sides of the pot, allowing the potting mix to retain moisture longer. Plastic is inexpensive, lightweight, and comes in all colors, shapes, and sizes. Recycling water jugs, juice bottles, and other containers into planters is another way to use plastic for plants. It is easy to clean and disinfect.

Wood

Wooden planters offer an affordable and versatile option for houseplants. Wood tends to be acidic and is a great insulator, keeping consistent soil temperatures. Wood absorbs water unless treated, allowing the soil to stay moist. Drainage must be excellent. If drainage is slow, drill more or larger holes in the bottom.

REPOTTING YOUR NEW HOUSEPLANTS

There are a number of reasons to repot a houseplant. Primary reasons are it might have outgrown its current container, a year or two has gone by since the last repotting, or the plant got smaller and needs to downsize its planter. Other reasons point to revising the soil composition and amendments, changing to a different planter, suspected root rot, or pest damage.

When repotting, always start with fresh soil and sterile equipment so you don't transfer bacteria, pest eggs, or disease from other situations. For houseplants other than indoor trees, please only make a 1- to 2-inch increase in planter size because the roots will only access the water within their reach. As mentioned earlier, tall and deep pots must be reserved for larger, more robust plants with a larger root mass.

Soil Preparation

Best practices dictate using predetermined ratios of various commercial potting mixes to create customized planting mediums for different types of plants—don't forget to research your plant's requirements.

Prebagged, pre-mixed commercial potting soil is a fantastic base to use in creating the perfect potting medium for your plants. Get to know the compositions of the specialized mixes, as they can be used for amending potting soil without having to buy quantities of bark, sand, and peat moss for DIY mixes.

For instance, adding commercial cactus mix to regular indoor houseplant potting soil incorporates sand and drainage but not additional moisture-retaining properties. A ponytail palm or Christmas cactus would love this mixture. African violet commercial potting mix, heavy in peat, when added to regular potting soil, makes a super moisture-retaining mix. This mixture would be great for begonias. Orchid mix is mostly all bark; it makes a great amendment to regular potting soil by adding compostable drainage. At the very least, have extra perlite or vermiculite available to add to potting soil for improved drainage.

- Create a good all-purpose soil mixture to keep on hand for fast-draining soil: mix two parts premium potting soil, one-part African violet mix, and one part perlite. One recipe translation is two scoops of potting soil, one scoop of peat, and 1 scoop of perlite. Add a scoop of sand for succulents or bark for philodendrons and pothos.

Soil mixtures lose their structure, compacting over time. The organic materials are put there to retain moisture. But these amendments of compost, peat moss, Sphagnum moss and bark chips degrade over time into smaller particles; allowing the soil to compress tighter with every watering, leaving poor oxygen exchange and loss of air flow in the soil over the years. Trace elements also get used up.

Components that will not decompose, such as vermiculite, perlite, and coarse sand, keep the soil structure intact the longest. They all have excellent moisture retaining properties. These would be the best to have on hand for amending commercial mixes.

Sometimes there is trepidation about repotting. The steps are the same throughout the kingdom. Approach this task with plenty of time (it's finished quicker than you think), and have all the tools and supplies within reach.

Be curious! Typically, the chance to observe the root structure comes once every year or two. Healthy plants are resilient and take to repotting well, especially when their living conditions improve.

Here's how to remove the plant from its current planter. Put on gloves and use a tray, newspaper, sheet, or towel to catch the loose soil for easy cleanup.

1. Please resist the temptation of digging into the soil and pulling the plant out by its stem. (A rootbound plant will slide out easily, which is OK.)
2. Turn your plant sideways, gently place your palm over the soil with the base of the plant nestling between the fingers, and tap the bottom of the vessel with the other hand, while turning the planter upside down. Catch the plant and carefully lay it down or prop it up, with the roots closest to you, taking care not to break any stems. Propagate any stems that do break.
3. There is no need to loosen the soil/root ball if it is a healthy mix of roots and potting medium. The roots will quickly grow their way through the new soil of the larger pot. At the same time, there is nothing wrong with tapping the root ball to get some of the old, used soil to fall away. If there is a tight basket of roots, you may untangle what you can, or, snip ten to twelve roots around the side of the root ball. A root will branch out from where the snip was made.
4. Cover the drainage hole of the new pot with a section of nylon window screen. The screen will retain the potting mix when watering.
5. Dump some fresh potting mix into the empty planter. Fill any gaps by pressing or tapping the medium firmly.
6. Set your houseplant on the potting mixture, centering if desired. Position the plant's crown at the same soil level as it was before.

7. Fill the space with more potting mix, and leave room at the top for watering.
8. Gently tamp down the dirt around the base of your plant so it stays firmly upright.
9. Water thoroughly.

Here is a little story from my journey. In my earliest houseplant-parenting years, I was a repotting fanatic. Experimenting with various planter sizes, shapes, and styles, I matched (and re-matched) houseplants by correlating the size of their root structure to the planter size and shape. Some plants were repotted a few times or until I was satisfied the match between the root ball and the planter was as good as it could get.

More importantly and at the same time, I became fascinated by amendment ratios. I was surprised to find that adding the right proportion of drainage amendments to a commercial potting mix makes a world of difference in growth rates. I learned that a well-draining, properly amended potting mixture eliminates leaf yellowing due to wetness.

Vermiculite was my favorite soil additive for aeration and drainage. Today perlite, bark, and sand are the most common aeration amendments, with peat and Sphagnum moss used for water retention. I can't stress enough to pay attention to the plant's requirements.

I also gave up using pebbles, stones, and shards of broken clay pots in the bottom of my planters. Using them caused drainage and bottom-watering issues by creating large air gaps. Now I know they also create the ideal living space for fungus gnats to set up shop and breed in.

The play between air and water is elementary; air bubbles up through water. The layer of pebbles in the bottom of the pot allows for large air spaces to form. When watering from the top, the air from these large spaces bubbles upwards against the water, slowing down the rate of drainage. Air pockets can form around the roots and prevent areas in the soil from getting moisture. Bottom watering becomes ineffective; water does not jump the air gaps to wick effectively.

I have found success using a flat nylon barrier, usually a piece of window screen or craft cloth, between the soil and the drainage hole. This practice eliminates air gaps which allows for quicker drainage, makes bottom watering effective, keeps the soil in the planter, and denies fungus gnats a home.

SURVIVAL TECHNIQUES THAT GO THE EXTRA MILE

The advice in this section comes from years of experience with houseplants. It's the kind of advice you'd get in a houseplant meet-up or talking to a veteran of houseplants during a visit to the nursery.

During my excessive repotting stage, I realized that putting one houseplant into a large planter in hopes it would grow huge (because I wanted large, impressive houseplants) did not achieve my goal. To create large, impressive houseplants in short order, crowd six, eight, or ten propagated pieces of the same plant into a 6- to 8-inch pot or go to a larger planter with more rooted cuttings.

For climbing vines, add the pole before the plants are added. Strap the plants with hook and loop tie-wraps to the pole as they grow to allow for repositioning and vine growth. Twine also works well for tying up vines.

Happy houseplants are in planters just slightly bigger in circumference than their roots can reach. Some plants even prefer snug roots, such as African violets and snake plants. Tropical houseplants grow faster with fewer problems when the roots are contained in a size-appropriate planter with a properly aerated potting mix and excellent drainage.

Consider transplanting down as well as up. When moving to a smaller container, or wanting to repot into the same planter, prune no more than one third of the roots off. Start pruning at the bottom with the curled root-bound area or the tip ends and work upwards, then inwards slightly. Never take off roots emerging directly from the stem area. Prune the top-growth foliage accordingly, after the plant is settled into fresh soil. Use top trimmings for propagation.

It's better to start with a low-maintenance plant that won't require all your time and attention. A plant doesn't have to be complicated to be beautiful, and several species will decorate your house while demanding little from you. The transition to fussier plants will happen naturally.

Underwatering

Understand what underwatering means. Underwatering does not allow the entire potting medium to get saturated at once. It does not refer to the time between thorough regular watering. Underwatering takes a few forms. It can be watering sporadically in small amounts (emptying the last dregs of a bottle of water into the closest houseplant), adding only enough water to wet the top third or less of the planter, watering one side of the planter, or watering just enough that little to no water comes out the bottom of the pot.

Over time, underwatering eventually spells death to a potted plant. You may be cruising along for weeks, months, or an entire season, doing just fine with your particular choice of underwatering method, until one day, the houseplant is limp, and the leaves start turning yellow in distressing quantities, even after recently administering the usual minimal water ration. Or, the soil suddenly becomes so desiccated that water runs past it. Sometimes the soil ball floats out of the pot. In any case, your plant may look ready for the compost heap. Just submerge the entire pot for up to an hour to rehydrate the soil. You may be surprised at what happens next.

There is a point of no return when underwatering or forgetting to water a plant. When a plant gives up the ghost, salvage the pot and try again.

Water Properly

Be generous when watering, but avoid saturating the potting medium too often in a short period. Give the soil a chance to dry and refresh the oxygen to the recommended level for the plant species: when the top inch is dry, when the top half of the soil mixture is dry, or when the entire pot is as dry as a tightly wrung sponge, and so on. In any case, ensure proper drainage to prevent waterlogging.

Let water drain through the potting mix into the cache pot and let the plant sit there for up to 15 minutes before emptying, although the excess water can be emptied right away. Alternatively, take the plant to the sink and water thoroughly. Think of Mother Nature opening up the rain clouds so the soil gets completely saturated. Even the deserts (cacti) get a good soak occasionally. Soaking and drenching rehydrates the potting soil and floods out air pockets. It would be best if every plant gets watered completely through and through at least once a month during the growing season. The trick is letting them dry out to the right level of dryness before watering again.

For faster watering, use a cache pot or basin with water in it to sit the planter in while water is added from the top. As air pockets escape up through the top water, more water is sucked up at the bottom through the drainage holes.

Invest in a watering can explicitly designed for houseplants so water gets directed to the soil, all around the pot, and does not splash on the leaves. Watering plants with bottles or drinking glasses can result in uneven water distribution and make a mess. Get a watering can with a long spout and a small opening. The small spout opening will ensure slow watering, which is conducive to thorough watering.

Be resigned that watering can be the messiest aspect of tropical houseplant care. On watering days, sling a towel over one shoulder, grab an empty bucket (to pour runoff out of the cache pots into), the watering can, and commence watering. To save even more steps and time, strategically hide water jugs of prepared conditioned water near groups of plants. Use these reservoirs to refill the watering can.

Remember, depending on the species, allow the necessary drying-out period before watering thoroughly again. Finding the right balance of dryness and total drenching is the key to watering, with few exceptions. Be flexible with a watering schedule.

Invest in a good moisture meter with a probe to become trained at analyzing the dry state of the soil and potting mix. Lift the pot and get a feel of the weight before and after watering. Follow the guidelines of how much moisture the plant likes to live with for the majority of the time between watering. With practice, you will soon know when to water without using a water meter.

Fertilizing

Feed your plants! Please use fertilizer if the documentation for that houseplant calls for it. Some houseplants require heavy feeding while actively growing. Some plants do not tolerate commercial fertilizers as well as they tolerate the milder fish emulsion. Some houseplants do best with only compost added as a source of nutrition and will die from commercial fertilizer.

Healthy heavy feeders use the available nutrients in fresh potting soil within months. Even a diluted amount of a common commercial fertilizer can make a noticeable difference in the growth rate these houseplants exhibit.

Succulents in general do not tolerate commercial fertilizers well and will, at most, only take a very diluted solution of fish emulsion. I rely on a yearly repotting for succulents, adding compost to the fresh potting medium.

Beneficial amendments that feed the soil are compost, worm castings and soil infused with mycelium or mycorrhizal soil. Do not be surprised or alarmed to see a few mushrooms if you use mycorrhizal soil. Do not use garden soil.

With all plants, I recommend fertilizing after watering while the potting mixture is still damp to help prevent fertilizer burn.

Bonding

Talk to and connect to your plants. It is scientifically proven that plants react to the surrounding environment, whether it is people's voices or music. Plants can absorb the sound vibration around them. They will grow bigger and healthier when the noise is calm and relaxing. The carbon dioxide expelled from humming, singing, or talking to your plants benefits the photosynthesis cycle.

Observe your plant regularly. Take notice when any changes happen with your plant, for the good or the bad, and make a note of it for future reference.

Propagating

Propagation methods vary from plant to plant. Depending on the season, roots can take over a month to develop. Take cuttings between late spring and early summer for the fastest root development, although anytime will do. Understand that not all cuttings or propagation attempts will be successful. Stay encouraged despite this fact; start more than one cutting if possible.

Newly propagated roots grow from the stem nodes. A stem cutting may have numerous nodes submerged in water or a damp medium of moss or potting mix for propagation. Be wary of allowing the bottom leaves of a cutting to sit in water, which leads to rot.

The standard propagation technique asks for stem cuttings to be 2 to 6 inches long, ending below a node. Ideally, each cutting needs at least one growth node and two to four leaves at the top. Cuttings will not root without a node, but leafless stem cuttings may produce a new plant.

Water propagation is common and effective for many houseplants, although not all. Place the cuttings in water. Change the water frequently. Exactly how often the water gets refreshed will depend on your schedule and the type of vessel you're using. However, best practice dictates changing weekly to provide fresh oxygen to the roots and prevent the water from stagnating.

Using an opaque container prevents algae growth and provides darkness to the roots, but using a clear glass vessel allows you to monitor the propagation progress and watch the roots grow. Either way works. Plant into a prepared soil mixture when the roots reach at least an inch in length.

Some plants will live indefinitely in water. Fired clay balls may be used as a substrate and anchor in conjunction with water propagation. Add small quantities of nutrients to the water for aqua culture.

Alternatively, stick the node end of the cutting into a shallow pot of moist, sterile potting mix. Place this in bright, indirect light, and monitor the moisture levels.

Situating the pot inside a clear bag or bin to maintain humidity levels increases success. The cutting will have a lower chance of rooting successfully if the soil is not moist enough, but it may develop stem rot if it is too wet. Leafless node cuttings can root successfully with this method. This method does not have as high a success rate as water propagation.

Instead of soil or water, you can also opt for the air layering method with Sphagnum moss. (Unlike its deceased dark brownish-black relative, peat moss, Sphagnum moss is green in color and is a live moss with active, living cells.) Soak the Sphagnum moss in water, wring out the excess, and use this damp Sphagnum to loosely wrap a stem where a shallow cut was made under a node with a sterile razor knife. Secure plastic wrap around the damp moss to keep the whole thing moist. Watch for roots to develop. Once present, finish cutting the stem below the new root growth and plant the cutting.

Dividing multiple plants from one pot into separate containers counts as propagation, as does removing offshoots that grow out from the base of the mother plant.

Tool Arsenal

Extra tools are not necessary for success, but they can help. Having dedicated supplies in one place makes it convenient to tend the houseplants. Consider these:

- nitrile gloves or gardening gloves to protect skin from toxins
- herb snips for pruning
- rooting hormone powder for propagating
- large spoon, ladle, cup, or scoop for moving potting mix
- floral wire cut into pieces for pinning vines to the soil
- wooden skewers and small hair claws for propping up leggy growth
- twine or hook and loop tape for tying up vines to a support pole
- extra jars, bottles, or vases for water propagation
- extra cache pots and drip saucers
- a bucket to empty cache pot water into when watering
- dish towel for water cleanup
- hydrogen peroxide (3% H_2O_2) as a soil drench

- vinegar or bleach for disinfecting tools
- a magnifying glass
- dedicated measuring cups and spoons for insecticides
- spray bottles for solutions and misting
- newspaper or a sheet to use during transplanting
- watering cans
- moisture meter

COMPANION PLANTING FOR HOUSEPLANTS

Houseplants can look beautiful independently, but having a dedicated space for several plants will make your home environment more pleasing. Companion planting means growing plants near each other in different pots or in the same pot. Plants enjoy company, and combining similar plants will make it easy for you to care for them simultaneously.

Grouping plants from the same genus often works in companion planting since their needs are similar or match perfectly. Choosing by genus can also help you identify potential companion plants, albeit different species.

A plant growing too fast could cause its companions to suffer. Pruning helps to control a rogue plant. Be flexible with companion planting and open to switching out plants or starting a group planter over from scratch.

Even with the utmost dedication and care, plants can still develop problems. That can be frustrating. In this chapter, we've seen how important it is to pay attention to detail. By going through it with an open mind, you may have identified some of the mistakes you've already made and found a solution you had never thought of.

Plants can show signs that all is not well. These signs will appear when the plant suffers from pests, diseases, neglect, poor water, or nutrient deficiency. In the next chapter, I'll show you how to identify and rectify those signs.

21iStock.com/Ольга Симонова

CHAPTER 3:
LOST IN TRANSLATION

DECODING YOUR PLANT'S DISTRESS SIGNALS

Like us, plants can get sick and require proper treatment to heal. It's essential to regularly inspect houseplants and take appropriate action to prevent or control problems before they cause serious harm to the plant. When you have several plants inside your home and one becomes unwell, that ailment could spread to the others. In that situation, the best action is to isolate and treat the unhealthy plant before reintegrating it with its peers.

For some people, diagnosing plants is the most frustrating part of this hobby. To me, troubleshooting these magnificent beings and giving them a new chance to grow and flourish is extremely rewarding. It takes time and patience but is entirely worth the dedication.

THE NATURAL LIFE CYCLE OF A PLANT

Common knowledge states that houseplants have a lifespan between 2 and 5 years, but they can go further. Your plants will not last forever, but don't have a specific lifespan.

The growth tissue of a plant is known as meristematic tissue and is found in several areas of the plant—stem nodes, flower buds, and roots. Growth can be primary, increasing the plant's height and length on its roots and growing tips, or secondary, increasing the thickness of stems and branches.

With some plants, you can pick a leaf and toss it on some damp potting mix, and it will sprout roots and grow into a new plant. That's because of the meristematic cells, which can change into different types of cells. This process is "perpetually embryonic" and allows for indefinite growth.

As a houseplant owner, you can do your best to give your plants the conditions that will allow them to grow indefinitely. Plants will live longer or shorter, depending on how well you care for them. Under ideal conditions, a plant can live for centuries.

Houseplants grow larger primarily through the hormone auxin in the meristem tip tissue. Pinching the tips of stems or vines removes the hormone's most significant concentration reservoir from the stem's end, enabling the lesser amounts of auxin in the rest of the stem nodes to activate, creating lateral growth. You can use this to your advantage by directing the development of your houseplants when pruning. If a plant grows too tall for your liking (or your space), you can cut it back, encouraging the plant to develop a bushier growth habit.

When the opportunity presents itself, practice resurrecting a plant from poor health. Results can be immediate, take a few months, or end badly. Whatever the outcome, gaining experience in this way instills more confidence.

Methods to nurse a plant back to health include:

- pruning the plant by trimming off dead or even live foliage
- propagating what is available
- dividing and repotting into a smaller container
- repotting with fresh new soil or potting mix
- Use conditioned water
- applying insecticides, fungicides, or remedial soaps
- moving to a brighter or dimmer area
- using a grow light for 8 to 14 hours
- covering the plant in a plastic bag (increases humidity)

I don't use the word commitment lightly. It's about more than watering your plants at the right time and giving them the right light. Sometimes you have to spend time with a plant, analyzing its leaves for yellowing or wilting, and figuring out how to solve a problem. Even plants that need little care will cry for help occasionally, and you need to hear it. That's easier said than done, but with practice and study, you will learn what each plant needs and how to help them last longer.

WHAT YOUR PLANT LEAVES ARE TELLING YOU

Here you'll learn how to analyze your plants and determine in what way they need your help. Knowing what optimal health looks like makes for a good starting place. Please take a moment every day or so and enjoy your plants by observing them, noticing new growth, touching the soil, picking up the planter to check the weight, and looking at the undersides of the leaves. Check your plants with a magnifying glass occasionally.

Brown Leaves

The main sign of drought is brown leaves. You can check the planter's weight by lifting it when they appear. If it feels very light, you might have to dunk the entire pot into a tub of water or drench it at the sink to ensure total soil saturation. This can be hard to do with large plants, but these are the ones that need it the most, because large indoor plants tend to require more water than small ones. A large potted plant may need more water to get the soil wet, but it does not need to be watered more frequently and can take a more protracted watering schedule than a small vessel.

Root Rot

Telltale signs of root rot are wilting, stunted growth, sporadic yellowing leaves and thinning of foliage.

If your plant's roots get black (or dark brown) and soft, it may have root rot, a serious issue that can cause the plant to die. Root rot does not happen overnight after watering. It comes from constant wetness. The decay will spread and cause plant tissue to collapse up to the stems.

With rotted roots, remove the pot—prune all of the bad roots off (they will be mushy or slimy) and repot the plant into fresh, freely draining soil. Apply a hydrogen peroxide drench monthly. Please ensure the drainage holes are functioning and not clogged. Use a smaller planter if the current planter is too large.

Stretching

When a plant needs more sunlight than it can get in its current position, it will stretch its foliage towards the light. Stretching is common during fall and winter but can happen in any season.

Consider moving the plant to a different spot, even a few days a week, to get the sunlight it needs. If a site like this doesn't exist in your home, turning on an indoor grow light for 4 to 6 hours can provide the necessary light.

Also, consider rotating the pot one-quarter turn every time you water so that the stretching, if minimal, occurs evenly as the plant grows.

Sunburned Leaves

Too much direct sunlight can burn your plant's leaves, making their tissue brown and crispy. A precursor to browning will be pale-colored leaves. Sunburned leaves will affect your plant's growth and keep it from photosynthesizing.

Removing the plant from direct sunlight is the first step, and the plant will recover with time. It would be best to prune the brown leaves, as they will never turn green again, and allow new ones to grow. Be careful not to remove more than one-third of the foliage at a time. Soak the soil if dry, allowing the roots to send more moisture to the leaves.

Sunburning can occur indoors when the seasons change from winter to spring, and the sunlight intensifies. Moving a plant outdoors to a sunny spot without transitioning from shade to sun can also cause sunburning.

Yellowing Leaves

Many factors can lead your plant to develop yellowing leaves. These can be hard to identify, but you can eliminate possibilities by changing the plant's routine, one aspect at a time. That includes giving it more or less light or more or less water. Use filtered water or conditioned water instead of tap water. Try placing it in other sites in the house with varying humidity levels. Review how much fertilizer your plant is receiving. Too much or too little of certain nutrients can turn the leaves yellow. After making a change, a day or so may go by before you observe a response.

After you determine what's causing your plant to suffer, you can go about rectifying it. Yellow leaves will not turn green again, so prune them off.

Note that if the yellowing leaves are exclusively located lower on the plant, they may be older leaves that are naturally dying off.

PESTS YOUR PLANTS NEED PROTECTION FROM

Remember to isolate houseplants for close inspection when you bring them home. The only way to get pests into your home is if they are introduced. Often, it will take a combination of tactics to manage an infestation.

Introducing natural predators to control pests needs some forethought. There has to be a way to sequester the plant and the beneficial control together. Consider using natural predators if an enclosed, lighted plant cabinet or large terrarium is available. Otherwise, ladybugs and other beneficials will fly around exploring. Turn them all loose outside once the infestation is gone.

Physical removal and using natural predators like ladybugs are only partially effective and work best in conjunction with organic treatments. Common houseplant pests include (How to Spot 6 Common Houseplant Pests, 2023; Fresh, 2021):

Aphids

Aphids can damage a plant's foliage and growth. They live on the undersides of leaves, on stems, and at the nodes sucking precious juices out of the plant. Aphids also create honeydew, which can grow mold and attract other diseases. You can remove aphids with a simple stream of water spray or any commercially available insecticide spray. Neem oil is a natural control method that disrupts the aphid's life cycle. Ladybugs eat aphids.

Fungus Gnats

Fungus gnats feed on a plant's roots and the decaying material they find in the soil. They can make the roots rot and harm the plant's growth. They make their homes in the top few inches of organic material of potting soil, drains, and the drainage holes of planters.

To deal with fungus gnats, you can purchase granules of a beneficial bacterium called Bacillus thuringiensis israelensis (BTI), commonly used to kill mosquito larve. When soaked in water, these granules release their main ingredient into a solution that will break the gnats' life cycle for good by killing off the larvae and pupae. Drench the soil with this solution. The bag will have instructions to help you reach the proper concentration. Bright yellow sticky traps work to catch the adults, but never fast enough, and never all of them. Use a plug-in insect light that is the size of a night light made to attract gnats.

One spring, I purchased a new bag of potting soil infested with fungus gnats. Without noticing the pest problem while outside repotting houseplants, I introduced the beasts into my home. The infestation continued after trying the yellow sticky tags and allowing the planters to dry out completely (common antidotes). I resorted to sequestering all my tropical houseplants into the garage and setting off a bug bomb. All the adult fungus gnats died. I next used an application of the BTI solution as a secondary line of defense against the larvae. The bug bomb and BTI application together eradicated my fungus gnat issue.

One way to use the insecticide approach on a smaller scale, employs a topless box, a large garbage bag, flying insect spray and the BTI bits. Put the box inside the garbage bag, making sure the bag will close over the top of the box and the plant. Place the infected planter in the box, spray the insect spray on the outside of the box avoiding the plant, and close the bag to create a fumigation chamber. After an hour or two, remove the planter and apply the BTI drench to the eradicate the larvae and pupae in the soil.

Neem oil is an organic insecticide and will work at controlling fungus gnats. Carnivorous plants, such as the sundew, will catch adult fungus gnats, but the larvae in the soil must also be eradicated.

Mealybugs

Like scales and aphids, mealybugs feed on plant sap, have a waxy coating, and secrete honeydew. Female mealybugs lay and hatch their eggs into a white material with the consistency of cotton. Mealybug infestation leads to yellowing and dying leaves and has an awful impact on plant growth. Their favorite plants are gardenia, poinsettia, hoya, jade, and coleus, but they can be opportunistic to other species. Neem oil is most effective. The oil coats them, leading to suffocation. Adding vegetable oil to insecticidal soap also works well. Apart from sprays of insecticidal soap or neem oil, fight them by dabbing them with a cotton swab soaked in rubbing alcohol. Lady bugs are not very keen on mealybugs due to their waxy coating.

Scales

These tiny crawling (when young) insects feed on plant sap and can be found on the underside of leaves, stems, and sometimes on leaves' surfaces. They are hard to see, and their favorite types of plants are figs, ivy, and citrus, although once again, they can be opportunistic and feed on other species. Adults have a waxy coating and create honeydew that can attract ants and fungi and grow mold if not rinsed. They resemble light brown or dark beige oblong spots. Controlling the younger ones with insecticidal soap or neem oil will have varying effectiveness, depending how young and soft the body is. Still, the adults need manual removal. Scrape adults off without damaging the plant tissue.

Spider Mites

Spider mites aren't always visible and can linger on your plant. They leave nearly-invisible webbing behind, hence the "spider" moniker. Their presence can result in foliage yellowing. Fight them with a soap and water spray, neem oil, or dabbing with cotton soaked in alcohol.

Thrips

Thrips bite a plant's surface like tiny vampires and suck its juice. They are hard to see due to their brown color and small size, but their damage to the plant is visible, often along the underside of veins and the edge of a leaf. The best way to eliminate thrips is to prune the leaves they've settled into. Insecticidal soap and neem oil are also efficient to some extent, but they do not completely eradiate severe infestations. Spot them with a magnifying glass.

Whiteflies

These pests like to feed on the sap in plants or leaves, which causes leaves to turn yellow and sometimes even white. Wilting may also occur. A persistent pest, whiteflies succumb to using a combination of different methods, including neem oil, insecticidal soap, or petroleum-based oils. Use yellow sticky traps to catch the adults. Ladybugs love to eat whiteflies.

COMMON HOUSEPLANT DISEASES

To know how to treat a bacterial, fungal, or viral disease, you must first recognize the symptoms correctly. Here are some of the most dangerous ones:

Anthracnose

Caused by the fungus Colletotrichum gloeosporioides, anthracnose usually starts its attack on the leaves and then onto the branches and stems of your plant, hampering their growth. You can identify it by a sunken yellowing or browning area, which evolves into the yellowing and browning of the entire leaf, then death. It's advisable to prune affected leaves or drastically dispose of a sick plant into the trash. A copper-based insecticide is efficient on this fungus.

Bacterial Leaf Spot

Look for black areas with a yellow ring around them. It could signify a bacterial leaf spot if these areas feel wet to the touch. You must find this while the spots are still isolated on the leaves, so you can remove the leaves before they spread to the rest of the plant. Dispose of pruned leaves into the trash, not the compost.

If the infection spreads to the entire houseplant, you might have to sacrifice it entirely. Bacterial infections are a severe issue that can harm your other plants. Nobody likes to remove an entire plant from the collection and toss it, but it's better than letting the bacteria spread. Sterilize the pot with a hot water and vinegar solution or bleach before reusing it.

Fungal Leaf Spots

You may find strange spots on your plant's leaves caused by fungi. These spots could be black, brown, yellow, reddish, or tan, distorting the leaves. Fungal leaf spots happen mostly in cool and wet environments and develop in the damp foliage and the potting mix.

Start by removing the affected leaves and the foliage debris that has fallen in the pot. Then apply a fungicidal spray to get rid of the rest of the fungi. Water your plants in the morning.

Gray Mold

Under certain conditions, the fungal disease known as gray mold can kill your plant. It disperses through the air in spores and can infect several plants simultaneously. When watering plants with gray mold, you may accidentally splash water on the leaves and flowers, spreading the mold around the rest of the plant.

A plant with gray mold will have brown spots on its leaves and flowers, preventing the latter from blooming and reaching their full growth potential. Treating the plant as soon as possible—applying fungicide and pruning the affected leaves and flowers—is the best way to prevent it from spreading.

Powdery Mildew

This fungal disease comes from oidium fungus; its spores travel easily through the air and thrive in low temperatures and high humidity (especially during wintertime). Powdery mildew won't kill your plant, but it will harm the plant's growth, not to mention its beauty. Begonias, African violets and some ferns may be prone. You can avoid this disease by not using overhead watering, circulating the air with a fan and lowering the humidity of the environment. Try not to let water touch the leaves when watering.

Sooty Mold

This mold isn't here for your plant but rather for the honeydew brought by other insects. Therefore, sooty mold will only come to your plants if they already have aphids, scales, or mealybugs.

Sooty mold harms plants by covering their leaves in black mold and preventing them from photosynthesizing. Despite looking ugly, it can be helpful, because it warns you about the other pests infesting your plants. The best thing to do is wash the plant with disinfecting products, wipe the leaves with a damp cloth, and treat the underlying infestation.

Viruses

These are the most insidious enemies of houseplants, for they have no treatment and spread quickly. A plant will show signs of viral infection in the color and shape of flowers and leaves; viruses create brown rings and mosaic textures in the leaf surface, cause unhealthy leaf growth, and prevent the entire plant from developing correctly.

Viruses can be hereditary or transmitted via unclean garden tools and pests like those we've just discussed. Toss plants contaminated by viruses into the trash bin. Sterilize the pot with vinegar or bleach before using it again, and sterilize your tools between uses by wiping them with an alcohol-soaked cloth.

White Mold

The saprophytic fungus causes this mold. It will cover the surface of the potting soil, giving it an unpleasant white and fluffy appearance, but it won't threaten your plant's health. You can remove the mold by scraping it off, but that will only make a cosmetic difference. It's better to reevaluate the kind of care you're giving to your plant. White mold can indicate that your plant's conditions aren't the best; it thrives in damp, low-light conditions and likely means overwatering, improper soil aeration, too large a pot for the plant, or insufficient light. Repot with a fresh well aerated potting mixture.

MEDICINE KIT TO HAVE ON HAND

You cannot tell when your plant is going to fall ill. This first aid kit will help you fight insects, fungi, and other nasty plagues that can harm and kill your plants. Use these solutions at your discretion, or as a preventative so you won't have to deal with infestations.

Copper Fungicide

This liquid copper and water mixture is one of the most efficient fungicides. Still, use this fungicide cautiously since copper is a toxic metal that can impact your plant's health. You should apply it before the fungus is visible—it will not work on existing infestations. Make a solution of 1 to 3 tablespoons of liquid copper to 1 gallon of water, spraying all over the plant and repeating it every 7–10 days (Dyer, 2022).

Horticultural Oil

Common horticultural oils are petroleum-based or plant-based. They are specifically formulated to target and control a variety of pests by disrupting their respiratory systems, and work through suffocation. Some examples are mineral oil, soybean oil and canola oil. Neem oil is considered a horticultural oil.

Isopropyl Alcohol

Most homes already have this available. It is useful for sterilizing tools and to prevent the spread of insects and diseases. Apply with cotton swabs when attaching insects.

Neem Oil

Neem oil is a vegetable oil derived from the seeds of the neem tree (Azadirachta indica), native to India. It is used as an organic insecticide and fungicide worldwide and in traditional medicine for various purposes. The oil contains compounds with insecticidal and antifungal properties that are toxic to some pests and help protect plants from disease. You can apply it directly to the leaves of plants or soil as a foliar spray or soil drench to protect the roots. This is my first line of defense remedy and I use it as a preventative.

Organic Insecticidal Soap

The chemicals in ordinary household soap can kill many pests that harm your plant. The most basic insecticidal soap mix comprises 5 tablespoons of organic soap in 1 gallon of water. You can also include vegetable oil for stickiness (1 tablespoon). Shake the bottle firmly to emulsify the oil into the mixture and apply.

ADVICE FOR KEEPING HOUSEPLANTS

In addition to what has been stated previously, here are some dos and don'ts when keeping houseplants.

Some Good Advice

- Add a handful of worm castings for every gallon of potting mix, as it prevents pests, adds good mycelium to assist the roots, and adds minerals back to the soil. It is very gentle and beneficial overall.
- Wipe the leaves of your tropical houseplants clean. That will eliminate dust, water, or fertilizer residue on the leaf surface, enabling photosynthesis.
- During quarantine, remove a new plant from its pot and check for abnormalities and new offshoots.
- Pick up smaller pots to gauge the weight and to get a closer look for regular inspection. Touch the soil and check for dampness.

Practices to Avoid

- Moving healthy plants around could harm their health. Only move plants to places with the same temperature, light, and humidity.
- Over-fertilizing is worse than under-fertilizing. It can harm healthy plants, so don't do it, even if your plant looks weak.
- Don't fertilize a newly purchased houseplant. The grower likely fertilized regularly to grow the plant for the market, and overfeeding it could kill it. Wait a few weeks before implementing a fertilizing schedule.
- Avoid exposing a houseplant to direct sunlight right away. Even though some plants require direct light, it's important to give them time to adapt. Ease them closer over time until they can take direct sunlight without burning.

- Be careful about allowing drafts of cold (or hot) air to hit houseplants. Keep them away from winter heat sources with low air humidity. Heat and low humidity tend to make a poor environment for tropical houseplants.

Don't feel guilty if you have to sacrifice a plant in poor health to save others from the same illness or plague. In some cases, quarantining the plant will work, but depending on the size of your home, the infected plant may still be too close to the others. Trashing the plant can feel drastic, but it's better to do it to one plant early on than to numerous houseplants further down the road.

I also hope my words have convinced you to treat and heal that plant with yellow foliage and rotten roots that you were thinking of getting rid of. Plants are living organisms, and while often discarded and replaced as inanimate objects, you can get a great sense of accomplishment and pride by bringing a plant back from the brink.

REVIEW PAGE FOR
THE TROPICAL HOUSEPLANT DOCTOR

Hey there,

As someone who has started reading The Tropical Houseplant Doctor, you already know the value of having lovely, thriving houseplants. But did you know that leaving a review for this book can also help others experience this same sense of fulfilment?

How often do you find the opportunity to help others? Whether it's through a kind word, a small gesture, or sharing your thoughts in a review, every act of kindness counts.

So, here's the ask: please leave an honest review of The Tropical Houseplant Doctor on Amazon. It's simple to do, and only takes a few moments.

To leave a review, head to the book's Amazon page and scroll down until you see the "Customer Reviews" section. Click the "Write a customer review" button, and share your honest thoughts. Feel free to post a snapshot or video of the book with your plants!

Thank you for considering this request and for being a part of the houseplant community.

Best regards,
Rhea

24iStock.com/Tanya Paton

CHAPTER 4:

BEGINNER'S LUCK

FINDING YOUR PERFECT HOUSEPLANT MATCH

Now that we've gone through almost everything you need to know about keeping indoor plants, it's time to talk about the plants themselves. More than just listing the family and genus species names, my goal is to inform you about how each plant functions and the simplest ways you can take good care of them.

Plants can last for a long time indoors if you respect them as living beings. Some plants are fussier than others, some will only look great sometimes, and some can need special care.

In the list below, you will find the best plants for beginners. They will likely endure in your home environment, even if you occasionally neglect their needs.

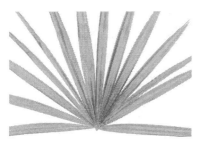
25istock.com/Rewat Patisena

Arecaceae: Rhapis excelsa, "Lady Palm"

The lady palm is a tropical plant with a graceful appearance and requires little care to become lush. It has a sturdy stem and dense green fronds arranged in an elegant fan-like pattern. Lady palms grow slowly but can reach up to 8 feet tall.

This plant enjoys being root-bound, so it must only be repotted every 3 to 4 years. After it's reached a height of 3 ft, you can top dress it instead of transplanting; to do this, remove the top 2–3 inches of soil and replace it with fresh soil. Be aware of roots near the pot's top (Lady et al.).

Lighting: Lady palms prefer bright, indirect light, and they work nicely indoors since they can also tolerate low-light conditions.

Watering: Lady palms require moist—but not drenched—soil for most of their growing season (summer).

Humidity: About 50%. Lady palms enjoy moist air by misting, or by using a room humidifier. Spider mites can appear if the air is too dry. Overly dry conditions will also cause browning on the tips of the leaves.

Temperature: 65–75 °F.

Soil: Moist, well-draining soil with high organic matter levels, such as peat-moss-based potting soil.

Fertilizer: Feed your plant monthly during the summer; not necessary in other seasons.

Propagation: This is done via seed and plant division with roots attached.

Toxicity: Nontoxic.

26iStock.com/Denise Hasse

Araliaceae: Schefflera arboricola, "Dwarf Umbrella Tree" or "Umbrella Plant"
Native to Taiwan, the Schefflera arboricola is also popularly known as the dwarf umbrella tree due to its dark green, glossy, umbrella-like leaves. It requires little maintenance besides regular pruning, without which it can grow up to 8 ft tall. Prune unhealthy or overgrown stalks to a height of 3–4 inches to encourage more compact growth.

Lighting: The dwarf umbrella tree prefers bright, indirect light but can also tolerate low-light conditions, making it a good fit for most indoor environments.

Watering: Water twice a week during hot weather, once a week during winter months.

Humidity: 50% and upwards.

Temperature: 65–75 °F.

Soil: Regular potting soil with a small amount of peat and sand provides good drainage.

Fertilizer: Feed 1–2 times a week during spring and fall. Wait about 8 weeks after repotting before starting a fertilizing routine. Fertilize newly-propagated plants once they have shown an inch of new growth.

Propagation: Do this via seeds or cuttings. Bury each stem cutting about halfway— for example, if the stem (not including the leaves) is 4 inches long, bury it 2 inches deep—in a moist potting mix.

Toxicity: This plant's sap can cause mild skin irritation in humans and is poisonous to cats and dogs (Baessler, n.d.).

27iStock.com/Tomas Llamas Quintas

Piperaceae: Peperomia obtusifolia, "Baby Rubber Plant"

Despite being unrelated to rubber plants, such as the Ficus elastica, the Peperomia obtusifolia earned the nickname "baby rubber plant" due to the thick, glossy leaves that give it a rubber-like appearance. It's a succulent-like variety of Peperomia; its spoon-shaped leaves store water and get plumper during periods of rain (or abundant watering). The spiky flowers of the plant are decorative, arrive on prominent stalks, and last a long time.

They don't respond well to repotting, and you should only do so if you can see the tips of the roots coming out of the drainage holes.

Lighting: Baby rubber plants require bright, filtered light, though they can endure medium indirect or direct artificial lighting.

Watering: This plant holds water in its leaves. Only water it when the soil is at least 80% dry—roughly twice a month, depending on your climate.

Humidity: About 50%. It will do well in slightly lower or higher humidity.

Temperature: 64–75 °F.

Soil: A well-draining organic potting mix enriched with perlite and some medium-sized chunks of bark will do wonderfully. Alternatively, mix in 10% succulent soil to help drainage.

Fertilizer: Once every couple of months (during spring and summer), apply a diluted but balanced houseplant fertilizer.

Propagation: Take stem cuttings (but be advised that they root slowly), or divide the offshoots from your plant.

Toxicity: All Peperomias are nontoxic to animals and humans.

28iStock.com/vspn24

Asparagaceae: Yucca spp. (Several Species), "Yucca"

Yucca plants make a statement when placed indoors. They can reach massive sizes, but their growth rate is slow; your yucca won't outgrow your space for a while. These plants are highly drought-tolerant, so you can forget to water them a few days after they are due for their regular drink—even wait a few weeks—and they will be fine. They feature a thick, woody stem and bladelike leaves reminiscent of agave. In nature, yuccas produce showy, cream-colored flowers, although they rarely do so indoors.

Lighting: Yuccas will do best under high artificial light (direct or indirect) or near a south-facing window.

Watering: Ensure that the soil dries out completely between waterings. In the spring and summer, water plants at most once a week; slow down to once a month in winter. Yuccas are sensitive to overwatering.

Humidity: Yuccas do not need misting or additional moisture; they are suited for desert life.

Temperature: 65–85 °F.

Soil: If it drains well; yuccas will do well in any sand infused standard potting soil.

Fertilizer: Use a liquid fertilizer monthly in the spring and summer.

Propagation: Divide offshoots from the mother plant or cut her trunks in half! Place the top leafy half of the plant into a container of moist potting soil, and it may grow roots. In time, the original plant will also regrow new leaves.

Toxicity: Toxic to animals and humans (Vanzile, 2023).

29iStock.com/Rj Ginting

Arecaceae: Howea forsteriana, "Kentia Palm"

A tall houseplant with lovely arching fronds, the kentia palm is easy to care for and requires little maintenance to survive. Bonus fun fact: Potted kentia palms were used as decorations on the Titanic, as they were a status symbol at the time.

Lighting: The kentia palm requires placement in a bright spot with indirect light.

Watering: In spring and summer (its growing season), water the palm when the top few inches of soil are dry. Reduce the frequency of watering in autumn and winter.

Humidity: 50% and upwards.

Temperature: 64–75 °F.

Soil: It appreciates nutrients but tolerates most soils if there is appropriate drainage. Potting soil mixed with sand or horticultural grit will do the trick.

Fertilizer: Feed the palm monthly with a liquid fertilizer during its growing season.

Propagation: Divide stems by pulling them apart at the root level. Include a few roots for each stem section.

Toxicity: Nontoxic (BBC Gardeners' World Magazine, 2021).

30iStock.com/Dwi cahyono

Asparagaceae: Cordyline fruticosa, "(Hawaiian) Ti Plant"

With glossy leaves in shades of bright magenta, this plant is a punchy addition to your home. Its leaves branch off a central stem; new leaves grow on top of the lower ones as those decay. It filters and purifies the air effectively.

Lighting: The ti plant prefers indirect light. Keep it out of direct sunlight.

Watering: Though drought-resistant, it develops better in consistently moist soil. During wintertime, it requires less frequent watering. The water quality makes a big difference, so opt for rainwater, conditioned water, or filtered water.

Humidity: 50% and upwards.

Temperature: 64–75 °F.

Soil: Get organic, fertile soil that drains well. Combine a potting soil with sand or perlite and add organic matter, such as compost or peat moss.

Fertilizer: During the summer growing season, apply a weak solution of liquid fertilizer once or twice a month. Do not use fluoride-containing fertilizers on this plant.

Propagation: Take cuttings with at least 3 inches of the clear stem (removing the lower leaves if necessary), and propagate these using your method of choice: water propagation, soil propagation in well-draining potting mix, or air layering with moist sphagnum moss while the half-slit stem is still attached to the mother plant.

Toxicity: The sap is toxic to humans and animals.

Araceae: Dieffenbachia spp., "Dumb Cane"

The name of this plant comes from its poisonous sap that contains calcium oxalate. It will numb your throat, burn your mouth, and possibly make you dumb (temporarily unable to speak) if consumed.

3iStock.com/Anant_Kasetsinsombut

Dumb cane leaves are creamy white to yellow towards the central vein and become dark green toward the edges. This shift occurs randomly within the same leaf, resulting in white, yellow and green patches and ribbons of color that come together along the leaf's body.

These plants come in two sizes: small, which can reach heights of 12 to 24 inches, and tall, which can reach heights of 6 ft.

Lighting: In nature, the dumb cane can grow in complete shade, but you will get better results if you keep your dumb cane in an area with bright, indirect sunlight. The more light you can give this plant, the more variegated and robust its leaves will be. In the shade, the leaves that form will be smaller and greener.

Watering: The top inch of soil should be moist, but be careful not to overwater it. Missed waterings won't harm your dumb cane plant, but prolonged neglect can cause the soil to dry out and its leaves to wither.

Humidity: 50% and upwards.

Temperature: 64–80 °F.

Soil: Blending equal parts perlite, orchid bark, and African violet mix would be a good potting soil option.

Fertilizer: Throughout the growing season, feed it with a liquid plant fertilizer once every 2 to 4 weeks.

Propagation: Cuttings root well in water. Additionally, cut a 3-inch piece of plant and place the cane section flat on sandy soil, node side down, and then partially bury it (leaving some of the cane exposed to light so it can photosynthesize). Keep the sandy soil moist at all times.

Toxicity: Toxic to animals and humans.

32istock.com/grace21

Poaceae: Dracaena fragrans, "Corn Plant"
The hardy Dracaena, or corn plant, has sword-shaped arching leaves that are dark green with a noticeable cream or yellow stripe running through the middle. These plants can grow 4–6 feet tall and 2 feet wide, with a single leaf reaching 2 feet long. If a corn plant becomes too tall, cut it back in the spring or early summer to control its growth. Wherever it's cut, a new cluster of leaves will grow.

Lighting: Although Dracaena plants can survive in shady, low light, they thrive in indirect bright light. However, keep them out of direct sunlight, or the leaves may burn.

Watering: These low-maintenance houseplants will put up with a lot, but do not overwater them. Keep the soil consistently moist but not soggy.

Humidity: 40–50%.

Temperature: Between 65–80 °F

Soil: It needs good nutrition. Two parts all-purpose, well-draining potting mix, 1 part compost, and 1 part sand is ideal.

Fertilizer: They only require fertilizer every 6 months. Be careful not to overfertilize!

Propagation: It's easy to control the growth of corn plants, as development occurs consistent with watering. In the spring or summer, take stem tip cuttings 4 to 6 inches long, and put them in moist potting soil.

Toxicity: This one is toxic to humans and animals.

33iStock.com/komargallery

Apocynaceae: Hoya spp., "Wax Plant"

Although the Hoya grows at various rates, it is one of the houseplants that flower! Its unique clusters of flowers are sometimes referred to as porcelain flowers because of their intricate detailing, consistent shape, and shiny exterior. The leaves also have a glossy, waxy texture, hence the nickname "wax plant." Given the right conditions, hoyas can bloom in the spring, summer, or fall. These have a trailing growth habit and can reach a length of 10 ft.

Lighting: While some direct sunlight is acceptable, protect plants from the hot summer sun. Hoyas can tolerate low light levels but won't bloom in them. They love an artificial grow light on a timer. Placing your wax plant 8 inches beneath the grow light and leaving the lights on for roughly 14 hours daily will help it grow and flower beautifully. It's vital, however, to provide these plants with a nap at nighttime. Please place them in complete darkness, as every beauty needs sleep and a break. Wait to move your plant until flower buds have developed on your plant.

Watering: Water from the bottom up by setting the entire pot in a tray of water and letting it absorb. This is a thirsty plant, but it doesn't enjoy sitting in moist soil. Water the plant during the winter with tepid water, just enough to prevent the potting mix from drying out completely.

Humidity: 50% and upwards.

Temperature: 64–75 °F.

Soil: Hoyas like a peat moss-based potting mix with ample drainage. A succulent blend with added peat also works well for hoyas.

Fertilizer: Feed your plant once a month in the summertime.

Propagation: Cut 4-inch pieces of vine, and remove most leaves from their nodes—keep one or two at the top of the cutting. Put pieces to root in water; once they have done so, plant them and keep them slightly moist for a month to help them adjust to soil growth.

Toxicity: All members of the Hoya genus are considered nontoxic.

34istock.com/Gogosvm

Asphodelaceae: Aloe barbadensis Miller, "Aloe Vera"

One of the most popular houseplants in the US, aloe vera is lovely and often used in beauty products and sunburn treatments. It also has a centuries-long history as a medicinal plant and is often used in health drinks. The plant has thick, fleshy, greenish leaves that fan out from the stem at the center. It looks stemless, but actually, it has very short stems. The leaf's margin is toothed and serrated.

Lighting: Bright, indirect light is best, but aloe vera can also take full sun. It does best in the south or west-facing windows but will grow leggy and pale in low light or shade.

Watering: Water Aloe thoroughly when the soil is dry, but as with most succulents, using moisture retaining soil is the biggest mistake. Err on the drier side.

Humidity: Aloe likes it on the drier side: 25–40% humidity.

Temperature: 55–90 °F.

Soil: Aloe vera likes well-draining potting mix, ideally succulent/cactus soil. If you want to make your own, use 40% perlite, sand, lava rock or all three mixed into potting soil.

Fertilizer: Like other succulents and cacti, aloe vera doesn't need fertilizer and is prone to fertilizer burns. Top-dress with a thin layer of compost.

Propagation: Separating offshoots from a parent plant is the simplest way to propagate this plant.

Toxicity: Aloe vera gel can treat skin conditions like burns and psoriasis. Some latex in the leaves can cause dermatitis or digestive issues if one is allergic to latex. Generally, the interior gel of the aloe vera plant is considered safe to eat, but latex is not. Aloe vera is toxic to animals. Ensure your plant is a true aloe vera before making aloe products: many similar plants in this genus are toxic to humans.

Keeping a digital journal of every plant you bring home will allow you to visualize your evolution as a houseplant owner. You can take pictures of leaves, roots, thermometer readings, and lighting conditions inside your house. Later, you can use those pictures to compare what you've been doing right and what still needs improvement.

People always do that with their pets and children, so why not do it with plants?

Speaking of pets and children, in the next chapter, I'll list ten plants that are safe for cats, dogs, and babies. Motivating your children to join in and help you care for these plants could spark a lifelong interest in gardening. Under your responsible tutelage and guidance, your little ones can grow up to become confident plant owners themselves!

35istock.com/Elena Grishina

CHAPTER 5:
SAFE AND SOUND

CHILD AND PET-FRIENDLY HOUSEPLANTS

Like many hobbies, gardening becomes more interesting when other people get involved. With children around, a fantastic opportunity arises for them to fall in love with plants, a passion they can carry on for the rest of their lives. It will teach them to be responsible, improve their confidence, and increase their love for nature. They will discover the science behind plants. At some point, they can have their own planter and the task of taking care of a houseplant.

Having cats and dogs should not discourage one from enjoying houseplants. These animals are curious, and it is impossible to control them constantly. Choosing plants that are not poisonous will ensure a pet-safe indoor garden.

37istock.com/Nickbeer

Asparagaceae: Chlorophytum comosum, "Spider Plant"

Spider plants are popular in households because they need little care. They only require deep watering once a week. Incorporate this into the children's routine to interest them in plants. Handling water seems more like fun than a chore, and tending to a growing plant and its dangling baby plantlets is exciting for all ages.

Spider plants are compact indoor plants that grow fast, even if neglected. They have long, narrow leaves which can either be solid green or variegated (green with white stripes).

Spider plants are also known as airplane plants and spider ivy. As houseplants, they grow as high as 20 inches, depending on the amount of light they receive and the size of the pot.

Lighting: Give a spider plant 6 to 8 hours of medium light and avoid direct sun exposure.

This plant produces babies on the side facing the light. Rotate the plant ¼ turn weekly to get a symmetrical display of little spider plants, or hang it in a bay window where it will receive light from multiple angles.

Watering: Keep the top 2 inches of soil dry, and water less frequently during winter.

Humidity: They do not require any extra humidity.

Temperature: 64–75 °F.

Soil: Potting soil with one quarter part added sand, perlite, or vermiculite for good drainage will be perfect.

Fertilizer: Using a liquid fertilizer diluted to half strength at the beginning of the growing season (spring and summer) will be most beneficial to the plant's health, but it is not necessary to ensure the success of your spider plant.

Propagation: This plant sends offshoots, called pups, from the mother plant on long stems. Cut these from the stem and plant them in moist compost or a glass of water.

Toxicity: Nontoxic.

38iStock.com/Photology1971

Arecaceae: Chamaedorea elegans, "Parlor Palm"

Give the home or workplace a touch of the rainforest with this hardy member of the palm family. Unlike most palms, the parlor thrives indoors under natural lighting and can offer up flowers (although they look more like berries). As houseplants, parlor palms reach a mature height of about 4 ft. They are slow growers and will only slowly outgrow their pots. Parlor palms are low maintenance, but keep away from windows, vents, and doors to avoid drafts.

Lighting: Bright, indirect sunlight.

Watering: Try watering once a week during its growing season—from spring to summer. In winter, it goes dormant and only needs watering once every 2 weeks (or even less often).

Humidity: 50% and upwards. Offering humidity and misting its leaves will benefit the plant's health.

Temperature: 64–75 °F.

Soil: Grow the parlor palm in a rich, well-draining potting medium for the best growth and performance. Most peat-based potting mixes work well, or amend every two parts standard potting soil with one part peat and one part perlite.

Fertilizer: Feed once every 3 months during the growing season.

Propagation: Grow from seeds.

Toxicity: Nontoxic.

39istock.com/GG

Bromeliaceae: Tillandsia spp., "Air Plants"

Air plants are a fantastic choice to grow indoors. They use their leaves to absorb nutrients and moisture from the air rather than the soil. Still, air plants do not get all the water they need from the atmosphere and can perish after a long period of dehydration.

Lighting: They grow in bright diffused light.

Watering: Soak air plants once a week (in a bowl or under a faucet) and then drain them by tipping upside down. Alternatively, water mostly through misting—spray the leaves every few days, and give it a deep soak once or twice a month. Either way, be careful not to allow water to accumulate in plant crevices, leading to rot and death.

Humidity: High, 50–70%.

Temperature: 50–90 °F. Air plants are sensitive to cold.

Soil: Air plants do not need soil to survive.

Fertilizer: Use a quarter strength Bromeliad food and mist or dunk, drain and dry. Do not fertilize in the winter.

Propagation: Remove the pups from the mother plant, and they will grow independently.

Toxicity: Nontoxic (Horton, 2021; Beck, 2023).

40istock.com/Akchamczuk

Acanthaceae: Hypoestes phyllostachya, "Pink Polka Dot Plant"

The pink polka dot plant's round, delicately downy leaves grow into a bushy shrub. The species can reach heights and widths of up to 30 inches under optimal circumstances if not pruned back. The polka dot plant will become fuller or bushier if it receives regular pruning.

Polka dot plants have pink, red, light green, and white spots on a dark green background. These plants stand out with their vibrant colors and the number of spotted or mottled patterns they show off. Some varieties have sharper contrast, with purple, red, and other deeper hues. They are heavy feeders and will need rich soil and monthly feeds.

Lighting: Bright light helps the pink polka dot plant to keep its vibrant colors. Put the polka dot plant a few feet away from a window and expose it to southern or western ight.

Watering: Polka dot plants need consistent moisture to thrive. The best way to achieve this is to plant them in rich, well-draining organic soil. When the top ¼ to ½ inch of soil has dried out, water it.

Humidity: 50% and upwards.

Temperature: 64–75 °F.

Soil: Polka dot plants favor organically rich, well-drained soil. These plants do well in an all-purpose organic potting mix.

Fertilizer: Use a balanced houseplant fertilizer once a month.

Propagation: Take stem cuttings and root them in water.

Toxicity: Nontoxic.

4liStock.com/isil terzioglu

Marantaceae: Calathea orbifolia, "Round Leaf Calathea"

The round leaf calathea is known for its broad, oval shape and light-green or silvery streaks on the underside. The attractive striped leaves add a different texture to any indoor garden. These streaks look particularly unusual, as they have the same patterns as a candy cane.

Calathea orbifolia is the largest plant of its genus. It can reach heights of up to 3 ft, with individual leaves reaching a width of 12 inches in diameter. The round-leaf calathea is a diva. Its maintenance is simple, although the temperature and humidity requirements need serious consideration. It is not considered a beginner's plant.

Lighting: The round leaf Calathea requires bright but indirect light.

Watering: Water every week or so when the top few inches of soil are dry. This plant is susceptible to overwatering.

Humidity: 50% and upwards. To achieve ideal humidity, place the pot on a tray of pebbles filled with water or use a humidifier.

Temperature: 64–75° F.

Soil: The soil should drain well and have a mildly acidic pH. Use a mixture of 1 part perlite and two parts peat for best results (as peat is an acidic medium).

Fertilizer: Calatheas prefer low-potassium, high-nitrogen fertilizers fed every month. Don't fertilize plants in their winter dormant stage.

Propagation: Use seeds or divide the offshoots from your plant when transplanting to a new pot.

Toxicity: Nontoxic.

42iStock.com/Khlongwangchao

Aspleniaceae: Asplenium nidus, "Bird's Nest Fern"

The bird's nest fern owes its name to the circular pattern of its leaves, which resemble a bird's nest. The glossy shine of these leaves requires constant humidity to maintain. They make quite a statement as houseplants.

Lighting: Indirect light or shade. Bright light can burn the leaves and dry out the plant. North-facing windows or artificial lights provide appropriate lighting.

Watering: Bird's nest ferns are very sensitive to chemicals in the water. Use a water conditioner product in the tap water. The soil mustn't dry out. Refrain from allowing the soil mixture to remain constantly soggy. Water requirement drops during winter, and you only need to moisten the soil every few weeks.

Humidity: High, 50% and above. These ferns thrive in bathrooms and kitchens, which usually have the most humidity.

Temperature: 50–72 °F.

Soil: Any soil with organic matter for an average houseplant will work for the bird's nest fern. Amend standard potting mix with peat and Sphagnum moss.

Fertilizer: Not necessary.

Propagation: You can find the bird's nest fern spores, which it uses to propagate, under its leaf fronds.

Toxicity: Nontoxic.

43iStock.com/imonpim Tangosol

Lomariopsidaceae: Nephrolepis exaltata, "Boston Fern"

The Boston fern exhibits graceful fronds that arch upward over the parent plant—an unusual feature that became the reason for its popularity. The Boston fern has tall, sword-shaped foliage, which only begins to arch as the fronds get bigger. Remove dead or browning leaves early to prevent them from falling onto the floor and soil surface.

This fern is a slow-growing species, like most other ferns. It can come back from near death quite well, which makes it an excellent option for beginners.

Lighting: Boston ferns require indirect/medium light.

Watering: It will grow faster if you keep it moist and soak the soil once a week. Let the top 2 inches of the soil dry out in between waterings in winter.

Humidity: 40% and upwards. Unlike the bird's nest fern, it can tolerate less-than-ideal humidity.

Temperature: 64–75 °F. It enjoys summer outdoors in temperate climates.

Soil: Use a peat-based potting mix with additional perlite for better drainage and compost for nutrients. Ferns prefer loamy, organically rich soil that drains well.

Fertilizer: Feed large Boston ferns water-soluble all-purpose plant food at least once a month during growing season.

Propagation: Divide out a clump of plants. Offshoots don't necessarily need roots, as they will root whenever they come into contact with soil.

Toxicity: Nontoxic.

44iStock.com/Sugeng Riyadi

Piperaceae: Peperomia spp., "Radiator Plant"

Peperomia plants come in many different varieties, such as the striped watermelon peperomia, the interesting textures of the ripple peperomia, and the "baby rubber plant" peperomia (which appears earlier in this book). Peperomias love warm drafts, unlike most houseplants, hence their nickname "radiator plants." They also make ideal desktop additions because they only require a little space.

Lighting: Peperomia plants like bright, indirect light. They can tolerate low-light conditions, which makes them splendid houseplants; they do not require direct sunlight to survive.

Watering: The main issue with these plants is overwatering, which can lead to leaves puckering and falling, eventually killing the plant. Let the soil dry out about 80% between waterings but don't overdo the restraint. Observe the leaves and water when they droop or dimple. Depending on climate and humidity, these can go without water an entire week or even a month.

Humidity: 40–50% and upwards.

Temperature: 55–80 °F.

Soil: Rich, well-draining potting soil is best for these plants.

Fertilizer: Although peperomias do not require frequent feeding, they will benefit from a liquid houseplant fertilizer once every two weeks in spring and summer.

Propagation: Peperomia plants can easily propagate in water: select a stem section with a leaf and change the water weekly.

Toxicity: All Peperomia plants are nontoxic.

45iStock.com/yuelan

Asteraceae: Pilea involucrata, "Moon Valley" or "Friendship Plant"

The most beautiful aspect of the friendship plant, also known as the moon valley pilea, isn't its flowers but its leaves, which feature a toothed texture and dark-red undersides. The leaves grow in pairs, opposite one another, and make the plant an excellent option for home decoration.

Friendship plants grow fast and wide; you must prune them to avoid excessive growth and to keep the plant compact. Their name comes from cutting off the growing tips of the leaves and offering them as a gift to a friend—those tips will root and become new plants that your friend can grow in their home!

Lighting: Keep the light low and indirect for this tropical jungle floor dweller.

Watering: Water moderately during the growing season but reduce watering from fall to late winter.

Humidity: 50% and upwards. The friendship plant's leaves can go brown with low humidity.

Temperature: 64–75 °F.

Soil: Friendship plants like a peat-based potting mix.

Fertilizer: Feed them once a month during the growing season using a half-strength dilution of regular houseplant fertilizer.

Propagation: Propagate via stem cuttings in water, moist potting mix, or division at the root level.

Toxicity: Nontoxic.

46iStock.com/gojak

Urticaceae: Soleirolia soleirolii, "Baby Tears"
This plant has tiny leaves in the shape of tears on the tips of long strings. With a fascinating texture, baby tears come in various colors and varieties. It makes an excellent choice for decorating terrariums that are open for airflow. The creeping stems of this evergreen perennial do best in constant contact with the soil. This plant is reasonably hardy and easy for beginners to grow. You can cut baby tears to any length.

Lighting: These plants prefer direct bright light. Baby tears will tolerate low light conditions but grow slower and somewhat leggy.

Watering: Whatever you do, don't overwater them. Err on the side of less frequent watering, once a week max.

Humidity: Very high, 75% and upwards.

Temperature: 64–75 °F.

Soil: Use a combination of 20% perlite and 80% potting soil for that perfect mix.

Fertilizer: During the spring and summer, feed your plant monthly with a balanced houseplant fertilizer. Avoid feeding the plant in the fall and winter.

Propagation: Divide the offshoots from your plant and plant them in small pots. You can also propagate stem cuttings in water.

Toxicity: Nontoxic.

Now that we've seen some examples of plants that won't harm your children and pets, it's time to look at the other side of the coin—plants with a higher level of toxicity that are nonetheless beautiful and could make a great addition to your home.

47istock.com/raksybH

CHAPTER 6:
DANGER ZONE

INDOOR PLANTS WITH HIDDEN HAZARDS

Knowing the toxicity levels of a plant is essential when you bring a new plant to your shared household. In this chapter, we will see some tropical plants that, despite their gorgeous looks, can be dangerous if not treated with respect. That shouldn't keep you from owning them, but taking precautions and maintaining these plants safely out of reach of children or pets is needed.

48iStock.com/Vasin Hirunwiwatwong

Euphorbiaceae: Euphorbia tirucalli, "Pencil Cactus"

The pencil cactus differs from most of its species by not having spikes. As a low-maintenance plant, it's a good choice for owners who travel a lot. The name "pencil cactus" comes from the cylindrical shape of its stem and branches, which make them look like pencils.

The pencil cactus isn't susceptible to common houseplant pests (except spider mites) and grows fast, reaching a 2–6 ft height and 1–3 ft width as a houseplant.

Lighting: The pencil cactus prefers to grow in full sun or direct light for at least 6 hours daily. It can, however, tolerate all-day indirect light.

Watering: This plant only needs to be watered a couple of times a month during warmer seasons and even less during winter. Water from the bottom up to avoid root rot.

Humidity: Low humidity, around 30%.

Temperature: 64–80 °F.

Soil: Nutrient-poor soil that is dry and sandy. Cactus mix works well.

Fertilizer: In the spring, fertilize your pencil cactus with a balanced liquid houseplant fertilizer once a year. It is not a heavy feeder.

Propagation: You can divide the offshoots from your plant. Let the cutting dry out for about a week to develop a callus over the cut end before planting. Lightly water a sandy potting mixture and set it in a sunny location.

Toxicity: Poisonous to humans and animals.

49iStock.com/Creative Style

Araceae: Epipremnum aureum, "Pothos" or "Devil's Ivy"

Pothos is one of the most common houseplants out there because it is one of the easiest to care for. It's a staple in offices, malls, and homes worldwide. It has trailing vines and slightly-pointed leaves. Some varietals, such as the neon green pothos, are a solid green color, while others feature splashes of color in white, green, yellow, or cream. Many variegated leaf colorations, such as the golden Hawaiian pothos, jade-and-pearls pothos, and snow queen pothos, are now on the market.

Lighting: Pothos performs well in low light but will grow more quickly with bright indirect light. If a variegated pothos plant does not receive enough light, the variegations will lessen, and the leaves may revert to solid green.

Watering: Water once every 1–2 weeks (depending on climate). Allow soil to dry out between waterings.

Humidity: 50% and upwards, but it's not fussy.

Temperature: 64–75 °F.

Soil: Standard potting soil is fine, as long as it's well-draining. It also tolerates soil mixtures that contain peat.

Fertilizer: Feed regularly while actively pushing out new growth.

Propagation: Take stem cuttings, ensuring they have at least one leaf and node, and stick them into water or soil. The nodes on pothos are easy to spot, as they often have aerial roots. You can also pin a piece of plant on the runner to the soil with a floral pin or wire.

Toxicity: Harmful to people and animals.

50iStock.com/Christian Steinsworth

Araceae: Philodendron hederaceum, "Heartleaf Philodendron"

It is said that the heartleaf philodendron is harder to kill than keep alive. Philodendrons form a large group, with the split-leaf philodendron (commonly confused with the Monstera deliciosa) being one of the most popular. It is similar in appearance and growth habit to pothos, but the leaves—which can grow up to 3–4 inches—are darker green and more heart-shaped. They grow fast.

It's best to keep the heartleaf philodendron, as with pothos, in hanging baskets or where they can trail. However, the sap irritates upon contact with human skin, so it's advisable to use gloves when handling it.

Lighting: The heartleaf philodendron is highly adaptable, performing well with little light, though it develops better with medium or indirect sunlight.

Watering: It can go for several weeks without being thoroughly drenched and appreciates misting.

Humidity: 50% and upwards.

Temperature: 64–75 °F.

Soil: Choose a potting mixture that contains peat moss, perlite, and any other soil types that retain moisture without becoming soggy.

Fertilizer: Whenever you notice your heartleaf philodendron sprouting new leaves, add some fertilizer to encourage growth.

Propagation: Increase plants using the floral pin method or root cuttings in water or in a moist soil mixture.

Toxicity: Poisonous to humans and animals (Combiths, 2022a).

Araceae: Spathiphyllum spp., "Peace Lily"

51iStock.com/Ludmila Kapustkina

Peace lilies are loved for their clean white flowers. Interestingly, what we think of as the flower is a modified leaf called a spathe, and the actual flower is the unassuming spike it surrounds.

Despite its name, this plant is responsible for several cases of home poisoning yearly. Its flowers, leaves, and stems contain calcium oxalate crystals, which cause mouth and throat irritation when ingested. Like most houseplants, peace lilies purify the air by filtering pollutants such as acetone, carbon monoxide, xylene, formaldehyde, and benzene (Baron, 2022). They also eliminate mold spores in the air, which can decrease symptoms of allergies and asthma.

Lighting: They prefer bright, indirect light.

Watering: Peace lilies can endure dry soil for a short time but prefer to be consistently damp. It is helpful to water them when the top inch of soil is dry (Daniel, 2021).

Humidity: 50% and upwards.

Temperature: 64–75 °F.

Soil: Use potting soil that is rich, loose, well-draining, and high in organic matter.

Fertilizer: Peace lilies are sensitive, so apply commercial fertilizer at half strength (diluted with water).

Propagation: It takes little time for peace lilies to fill a pot. These plants show indiscriminate growth if you keep repotting them to larger pots. You can propagate them during each repotting! Shake the roots gently as you pull them apart. Pick a shoot with at least two leaves and an independent root system. Peace lilies are highly sensitive to root disturbances, so be careful.

Toxicity: Poisonous to humans and animals.

Araceae: Zamioculcas zamiifolia, "ZZ Plant"

52iStock.com/Kseniia Soloveva

The stems of ZZ plants develop into an elegant, wand-like shape that begins thick and bulbous at the base and then tapers to a point. The fleshy, oval-shaped leaves line the stem. A shiny, waxy coating covers the entire plant.

ZZ plants get a bad reputation due to claims that they can cause cancer. Those cancer claims are not proven, although it's true that the plant is poisonous.

Lighting: The plant will develop better if you give it 6 hours of bright indirect light daily, although it can also tolerate lower light.

Watering: ZZ plants only require a thorough watering every 2 to 3 weeks.

Humidity: 40–50%.

Temperature: 60–75 °F.

Soil: ZZ plants enjoy good drainage; a mix of potting soil and cactus soil is ideal, as is soil that contains wood chips, perlite, or pumice.

Fertilizer: Fertilize every 6 months (or more frequently during the growing season).

Propagation: Taking stem cuttings is reliable, although ZZ plants can take several months to root in water.

Toxicity: Poisonous to humans and animals (The Sill, 2022c).

53iStock.com/Andrey Nikitin

Crassulaceae: Crassula argentea, "Jade Plant"

The jade plant is a succulent with beautiful paddle-shaped leaves. Jade plants are famous for their appearance, not needing much care, their easy propagation, and their adaptability for indoor growth. They can live for a long time and take readily to bonsai-tree-like forms.

Lighting: Go for bright, direct light. The jade plant will also do well in low light but will need less frequent watering.

Watering: Like other succulents, the jade plant stores water in its leaves and can go for a while without any water. Let it dry out completely between waterings, then water from the bottom up. Water when dimples occur in the leaves.

Humidity: Low, 30–50%.

Temperature: 65–75 °F.

Soil: Fast-draining soil, such as succulent soil, is best.

Fertilizer: During the warm season, you can apply a diluted succulent fertilizer every 4 months—check that it does not contain a lot of nitrogen.

Propagation: The jade plant propagates easily. You can remove a stem or leaf and bury the stem end in the soil, and a new plant will emerge. Before planting, allow the end of the leaf to callus over so it will not rot.

Toxicity: Poisonous to humans and animals (Jones, 2022).

Asparagaceae: Dracaena trifasciata, "Snake Plant"

With long, thin, upright leaves in assorted shades of green, snake plants are easy to identify and grow. There are over 30 varieties of snake plants, each presenting variations in leaf color and shape. Snake plants also absorb toxic compounds in the air, such as benzene

54istock.com/Prostock-Studio

and formaldehyde, which makes them a great addition to your home despite their toxicity. This plant, once known by the scientific name Sansevieria trifasciata was recently reclassified as Dracaena trifasciata.

Lighting: A snake plant will appreciate any light you give it but can thrive nearly as well in the shade as in bright sunlight.

Watering: Water thoroughly and then just let it dry out to 80-90% between waterings. Do not ever let it sit in water.

Humidity: Snake plants aren't fussy about humidity but develop better in dry climates.

Temperature: They aren't fussy about temperature, but anything below 50° F could harm them.

Soil: Snake plants require aerated and well-drained soil. Give preference to sterilized potting soil and add gravel, , or sand to help the air circulate.

Fertilizer: Use common houseplant fertilizer every 2 months during spring and summer.

Propagation: Water or soil propagation is best. Cut a leaf into sections and place the bottom side down into a damp soil mixture. The base portion of the entire leaf will sprout roots in water. It's also possible to do division propagation, separating smaller plants (pups) with their roots.

Toxicity: Poisonous to humans and animals (Snake Plants, n.d.).

55iStock.com/Wirestock

Strelitziaceae: Strelitzia nicolai, "Bird-of-Paradise"

The large, waxy paddle-shaped leaves of a bird of paradise join to a long, upright stalk. The flower looks just like a bird's head, and the colors are a striking orange with bits of blue. The flower is the most toxic part of the bird of paradise, though the entire plant has a mild level of toxicity. The flower is not likely to develop when the plant is indoors, but in case it appears, keep it away from children and animals.

Lighting: Bird-of-paradise plants require bright direct or indirect light. Rotate the plants to ensure all sides get equal amounts of light.

Watering: Make the soil moist but not soggy, and let it go nearly dry before watering it again.

Humidity: Very high, 70% or above. Bird-of-paradise plants like a humidifier or frequent misting. Keep the plants away from drafts.

Temperature: 65–85 °F.

Soil: Well-draining soil with plenty of aeration will help your bird-of-paradise thrive.

Fertilizer: Fertilize every 2 weeks except during the cold season.

Propagation: Cutting and planting a stem or leaf isn't enough for the bird of paradise to propagate—you'll also need to get a portion of the root.

Toxicity: Poisonous to people and animals (Bird of Paradise Care, 2019).

56iStock.com/in4mal

Araliaceae: Hedera helix, "English Ivy"

English ivy has aerial roots that can climb on a pole or a trellis and beautiful lobed leaves that look elegant in a hanging pot. You can choose among hundreds of varieties of ivy, which differentiate themselves through the color of their leaves. They can grow fast and will need repotting every couple of years. English ivy is poisonous when ingested, and its sap can cause skin irritation. Wear gloves when dealing with it.

Lighting: Go for constant bright light for success. Keep out of direct sun and shade.

Watering: Overwatering can affect this plant, causing its leaves to wilt and its roots to rot. Give preference to pots with many drainage holes in the bottom, which will keep the soil from becoming too moist.

Humidity: This plant likes 40% or more air moisture. English ivy needs cool and moist air to develop, away from drafts and heaters. Misting is beneficial, and it also helps to prevent spider mites.

Temperature: 50–75 °F.

Soil: This plant is okay with regular potting soil but will develop better in a rich, loose potting mixture with a high drainage level.

Fertilizer: Give monthly doses of a high-nitrogen water-soluble fertilizer all year, except for winter.

Propagation: Cut a piece of stem with aerial roots and root it in soil or water. Aerial roots can form fibrous roots.

Toxicity: Poisonous to humans and animals.

57iStock.com/Denise Hasse

Asparagaceae: Asparagus aethiopicus, "Asparagus Fern"

Despite its name, this is not a fern and is more closely related to lilies. This plant is popular due to its feathery foliage, which looks fantastic hanging from a basket. The asparagus fern can grow large indoors in bright light in a pot with excellent drainage.

Lighting: It can thrive in the shade but prefers indirect light.

Watering: Give it water every few days, keeping it moist but not soggy.

Humidity: 50%. This plant grows well in a moist environment. These like misting and a humidifier.

Temperature: 60–80 °F.

Soil: This plant requires loamy soil; potting soil with good organic matter will work well.

Fertilizer: Fertilize once a month during the warm seasons, using balanced half-strength fertilizer.

Propagation: You can propagate this plant by planting its berries or dividing and replanting its roots.

Toxicity: Poisonous to humans and animals (Asparagus Fern Care, 2021).

Flowers are the most visually stunning parts of a plant. That's not just a cosmetic aspect—it's an essential part of their evolutionary process. In the next chapter, we'll see ten tropical plants that produce stunning and unique flowers in all shapes and colors. Caring for plants can be an engaging process, and seeing the result of your efforts in blooming flowers can provide delicious satisfaction.

CHAPTER 7:

FLOWER POWER

BRIGHTENING UP YOUR HOME WITH BLOOMS

American poet Edwin Curran once wrote, "Flowers are the music of the ground, from earth's lips spoken without sound (Notable-quotes, 2022)."

Flowers have always carried an intense romantic aura and are present in our lives from the bride's bouquet to the flower crown at a funeral.

This chapter will show common indoor plants that produce beautiful flowers. Apart from their dramatic effect, these flowers indicate you're doing well with your houseplants. Seeing a bud appear and develop its petals is one of the most satisfactory parts of raising houseplants—and here's how to do it the right way.

58iStock.com/Raluca Ilie

Araceae: Anthurium andraeanum, "Anthurium" or "Flamingo Lily"

This plant has magnificent foliage and flowers in widespread colors. Anthuriums can bloom in red, white, pink, green, yellow, or burgundy (one color per plant). Anthuriums are perennial and can be grown outdoors in warm climates but do amazingly well indoors. Aside from humidity, it's not a fussy plant. The flowers will last for months if properly cared for. Due to the eye-catching flowers, this plant is sometimes called a "flamingo lily."

When planting, place the top of the root ball just above the soil surface. Repotting must happen every 2–3 years when the roots fill the entire pot; you can delay repotting by starting with a pot 2–4 inches larger than its current container so that the anthurium can expand.

Anthuriums can have trouble standing, so if your plant is bending too much, you can offer extra support with a garden stake or skewer. Secure the stem with a small hair claw spring clip.

Lighting: They do well in the shade but will develop faster under bright, indirect light. If you want your anthuriums to keep their pots manageable, it is a good idea to give them less light, which will slow down their growth.

Watering: Anthuriums require moist, but not soaked, soil.

Humidity: 50% and upwards. Regularly mist the leaves, avoiding the flowers, and wipe them with a damp cloth to keep them shiny and dust-free.

Temperature: 70–85 °F.

Soil: Peat-free multipurpose soil and soil-based compost or high-quality houseplant soil combined with orchid bark work best for anthuriums.

Fertilizer: In the spring and summer, feed once a month with a half-strength dilution of high-potassium feed (such as tomato fertilizer).

Propagation: Divide any offshoots from your main plant, or take a stem cutting with aerial roots, which will be forced to form fibrous roots.

Toxicity: Toxic to both humans and animals.

59iStock.com/Firn

Begoniaceae: Begonia maculata, "Spotted Begonia"

The spotted begonia is showy but low maintenance, providing beautiful pink or white flowers. It is sometimes called the angel-wing begonia for the shape of its polka-dotted leaves. The spots are silver-white, and the underside has a vibrant deep pink-red coloring.

Begonia flowers usually bloom during spring or the first part of summer. Once the flowers start to fade and wilt, you can grab the stem about a half-inch below the spent flower and remove it. This process, called deadheading, will allow the begonia to bloom again.

Begonias don't go dormant during winter, but they grow much slower during that season.

Lighting: The spotted begonia is a fast grower with indirect, bright light but also performs with shade. Avoid leaving it under direct afternoon sunlight, which can burn the leaves.

Watering: Let the top one inch of soil dry out between waterings, but keep the dampness in the soil. Given adequate humidity, begonias will only need watering weekly. Water less during winter and fall.

Humidity: 45% and upwards.

Temperature: 65–86 °F.

Soil: To encourage proper drainage, mix extra perlite into a richly organic potting mix.

Fertilizer: Every 2 weeks in the spring and summer, fertilize your plant with liquid houseplant fertilizer. Fertilizing more often with a half dilution of fertilizer will give your begonia larger leaves and promote the development of flowers. In the winter and fall, avoid fertilizing.

Propagation: Unlike most begonias, which have underground rhizomes and require root division, this is a cane begonia. You can divide it, but stem cuttings will root well in water. You can also use seeds.

Toxicity: Toxic to humans and animals.

60iStock.com/Jana Milin

Bromeliaceae: Billbergia nutans, "Queen's Tears"

This plant is nicknamed for its brightly colored flowers, which arch down gracefully, resembling tears. It is a type of bromeliad, which makes it similar in care requirements to orchids and air plants. It collects moisture from the air via its thin leaves, which can reach a length of 15 inches.

Lighting: Bright, indirect light is best. The plant will do well in the shade but will not flower there.

Watering: This houseplant can tolerate a missed watering occasionally. Keep the soil moist but never soggy. Never let the soil doesn't dry out entirely. The queen's tears are pickier about water quality than most plants: The fluoride and chlorine in tap water can make its leaves go brown, so it's best to use conditioned water or rainwater.

Humidity: Give them medium humidity of 40%–60%. This plant enjoys daily misting or moistened air, and the leaves will brown in drier environments.

Temperature: 60–75 °F.

Soil: Orchid soil is preferred, but you can simulate the ideal soil mixture with 2 parts bark and 1 part potting soil.

Fertilizer: In spring and summer, feed every 2 weeks with a balanced, water-soluble fertilizer. In fall and winter, fertilize once a month.

Propagation: Divide the offshoots or pups from your plant to plant elsewhere.

Toxicity: Nontoxic.

6listock.com/brizmaker

Primulaceae: Cyclamen persicum, "Cyclamen"

The cyclamen is known for its beautiful flowers that come in pink, white, and red. Its heart-shaped leaves are beautiful. Unlike most plants, its flowering and growth period is during winter and autumn. It dies back during spring and summer when it goes into dormancy. Instead of discarding the plant during this period, allow it to go through its natural life cycle, and it will bloom again the following winter. To keep the plant alive during its summer dormancy, place it in a cool, dark spot, water occasionally, and make sure its pot drains well.

Lighting: Cyclamen can't stand direct sunlight, which could kill them. Indirect light or shade both works.

Watering: Cyclamen is drought-tolerant, and overwatering will kill it. Reduce watering during summer, when it goes dormant—otherwise, water infrequently when the soil is dry.

Humidity: 50% and upwards. It does not tolerate dry air.

Temperature: 50–65 °F.

Soil: A porous, well-drained soil is preferable. Use an all-purpose, high-quality potting mix with horticultural grit (sand) and organic matter.

Fertilizer: For blooming plants, use a low-nitrogen houseplant fertilizer every month until the plant goes dormant, then stop fertilizing until it grows new leaves.

Propagation: Use seeds or divide offshoots from the main plant's rhizome. It would be best to wait for your plant to go dormant before dividing it.

Toxicity: Toxic to humans and animals.

62iStock.com/natalie_board

Orchidaceae: Phalaenopsis spp., "Moth Orchid"

One of the easiest orchids to grow, especially indoors, the moth orchid enjoys stable temperatures throughout the year. These orchids offer flowers in various colors and blotched or spotted patterns. If properly cared for, they can continue to bloom for months.

A moth orchid's active growth phase is spring to autumn.

Lighting: The moth orchid requires bright, indirect light. It doesn't react well to direct sunlight. You can place your orchid on a windowsill that faces east or give it artificial lighting.

Watering: Like most orchids, it's crucial to nail the watering, not making it too wet or dry. Try to keep it moist by misting weekly. Do not let the roots sit in water.

Humidity: 50% and upwards. Orchids respond poorly to moving. Also, avoid exposing them to radiators, heaters, or drafts.

Temperature: 60–86 °F.

Soil: Typically, a container filled with a well-drained bark mixture (orchid mix) works well. Plant in a bowl lined with sphagnum moss filled with orchid mix potting soil for a different look. Special orchid grow pots with side slits are available.

Fertilizer: Feed orchid fertilizer sparingly but consistently throughout the growing season. Use an orchid-specific fertilizer.

Propagation: Keikis are plantlets that occasionally grow on orchids. Watch for flower buds that begin to grow roots; these can be cut from the mother plant and planted in new containers.

Toxicity: Nontoxic.

63iStock.com/joloei

Gesneriaceae: Aeschynanthus radicans, "Lipstick Plant"

With long, trailing stems that can grow to 2 feet or more, the lipstick plant has waxy leaves and flowers that look like lipstick tubes when they open. Their color is usually red but can also be yellow, burgundy, or orange. Lipstick plants require a warm environment to thrive, which makes them a perfect fit for most homes. They look great hanging in baskets and are a fun curiosity to show your guests. Pruning them will make them grow fuller, and you'll only need to repot them if you see the tips of the roots coming out the drainage holes.

Lighting: Bright, either direct or indirect, light is required. It will produce more flowers the more hours of light you give it.

Watering: This plant likes soil on the drier side. Take it easy, and water only when the soil is dry.

Humidity: 50% and upwards.

Temperature: 65–85 °F.

Soil: Fast drainage is required, so add 1 part sand and 1 part bark to 1 part potting soil.

Fertilizer: Use standard fertilizer granules or slow-release granules for ornamental plants.

Propagation: Divide the offshoots from your plant or use seeds.

Toxicity: Nontoxic.

64istock.com/NNehring

Gesneriaceae: Columnea gloriosa, "Goldfish Plant"

It's easy to understand this plant's name when you see its tubular orange or orange-red flowers in the shape of a goldfish. The flowers aren't their only attractive feature—they also have beautiful dark green foliage with thick and waxy leaves. Pinching their growing tips will encourage new growth.

Mature goldfish plants bloom profusely during spring, summer, and during the rest of the year if you give them enough light. Your goldfish plant may require repotting to a larger container during spring.

Lighting: Goldfish plants like bright, indirect light.

Watering: Let the top 1–2 inches dry out between waterings. Slow down on watering during winter, but never let it dry out.

Humidity: 50% and upwards. Not tolerant of drafts.

Temperature: 64–75 °F.

Soil: Use a peat moss-based potting soil.

Fertilizer: Feed your plant every 2 weeks during the spring and summer using a water-soluble fertilizer diluted to half-strength.

Propagation: Divide the offshoots from your plant or use seeds.

Toxicity: It is slightly toxic.

65istock.com/artursfoto

Crassulaceae: Kalanchoe blossfeldiana, "Kalanchoe" or "Flaming Katy"

An exuberant succulent originating from Madagascar, the foot-tall stems branch to support softly scalloped round, fleshy emerald green leaves. Commonly found in grocery store floral shops with a profuse display of single or double small tubular flowers with flared petals, the blooms come in a rainbow of colors (red, orange, yellow) and display for a relatively long period of weeks to months.

Lighting: Place in a bright windowsill and offer bright indirect light.

Watering: Treat as a succulent and allow to dry out before watering. Water once a week.

Humidity: 40-50%.

Temperature: 60 °F -80 °F.

Soil: Cactus or well-draining soil works best.

Fertilizer: Only fertilize during the growing season with a ½ strength solution.

Propagation: Take a stem cutting and allow it to callus over. Place stem end into moist planting mix, and keep it moist until roots develop in 2 to 3 weeks.

Toxicity: Poisonous to cats and dogs.

66istock.com/Tharakorn

Oxalidaceae: Oxalis triangularis, «Oxalis Shamrock»

With purple, triangular, shamrock-like leaves, the oxalis plant will produce rosy-pink flowers during summer. Despite its appearance, oxalis is not related to clovers.

Lighting: Oxalis goes dormant during wintertime and sometimes in other seasons, but with consistent bright light, you may prevent this and keep its leaves around all year.

Watering: Let the top half of the soil dry out before watering again. This plant can tolerate slightly inconsistent watering.

Humidity: 40-60%.

Temperature: 65–85 °F.

Soil: Standard potting soil works fine for this plant.

Fertilizer: Use all-purpose fertilizer once every other month. When your oxalis starts to wilt, a good dose of regular strength fertilizer should get it back into shape.

Propagation: Divide the clump and plant the portions in different pots.

Toxicity: Toxic to humans and animals if taken in large quantities.

67iStock.com/kuzina1964

Gesneriaceae: Saintpaulia ionantha, "African Violet"

African violets have unique velvety leaves and pretty flowers that can bloom year-round and brighten any space. It may sound counterintuitive, but African violets enjoy being root-bound. When choosing a pot, select one that looks too small and ensure it has drainage holes.

Lighting: Direct sunlight will burn the leaves, so treat African violets gently with indirect sunlight—windows facing north or east are ideal, as are artificial lights—and rotate once a week to distribute light around the plant as they are prone to stretching.

Watering: Allow the plant to dry out somewhat before giving it more water. Avoid wetting the leaves and flowers, and always use tepid water.

Humidity: 50% and upwards.

Temperature: 64–80 °F. African violets don't enjoy the cold, so temperatures should not dip below 60 °F.

Soil: Use organic potting soil made specifically for African violets. Special wicking pots are available.

Fertilizer: Use a liquid fertilizer made for African violets. In the spring, summer, and fall, feed your plants every 2 to 4 weeks.

Propagation: Take a leaf cutting, ensuring it is mature, and propagate in water. You can also divide the offshoots from the base of the stem using a clean, sharp knife.

Toxicity: Nontoxic.

In the next chapter, we will see some plants that grow in the shade and require minimum light. That doesn't make them less appealing or less beautiful; on the contrary, they are very nice.

68istock.com/Thanabodin Jittrong

CHAPTER 8:
SHADY CHARACTERS

HOUSEPLANTS THAT LOVE THE DARK SIDE

Light is vital in plant development, but it might not be available in the necessary amount to raise certain plants. Perhaps the only room for plants is dark for most of the day. The windows could be facing the wrong direction. Alternatively, no windows exist where plants are desired. There are solutions!

This chapter highlights ten tropical plants that can be grown in low-light conditions. They are native to the rainforest, growing under the thick canopy of leaves formed by taller trees. These plants have developed broad, thin leaves to capture more light to survive in low-light conditions.

Plants that require low light also require less water, especially in pots 10 inches and larger. They need less care, can go longer between waterings, and will make a beautiful addition to even the darkest rooms. Low-light-loving houseplants grow more slowly.

69iStock.com/Reni Purnama Sari

Araceae: Scindapsus pictus, "(Silver) Satin Pothos"

Like its family member, the common pothos, the satin pothos is easy to grow indoors and very sensitive to cold weather. The satin pothos displays trailing heart-shaped leaves with a silky texture and silver patches, giving it a distinguished look. It does well on a bookshelf or in a hanging planter but can climb trellises or poles with its aerial roots. Satin pothos requires little maintenance, but pruning dead leaves will result in a healthier plant, and pruning the vines will prevent them from growing out of bounds.

Lighting: Satin pothos grows best in shade to indirect light.

Watering: Water thoroughly when soil is dry, approximately once a week, depending on pot size and climate.

Humidity: 40-50% humidity.

Temperature: 65–85 °F.

Soil: Any indoor potting soil will do.

Fertilizer: Water-soluble houseplant fertilizer can be used once every month during the growing season.

Propagation: A 4-inch cutting from a healthy plant can be placed in the soil and kept moist, or trailing vines can be pinned to the soil. It will root within a month. It also propagates well in water.

Toxicity: Mildly toxic to humans and animals.

Figure 70iStock.com/Mauricio Acosta

Marantaceae: Maranta leuconeura, "Red Prayer Plant"

This type of Maranta, or prayer plant, is so named because they fold up their leaves at night, resembling hands in prayer. Prayer plants are often confused with Calathea plants, which are related. A trained eye can differentiate them: the prayer plant does not grow as tall and has characteristic red veins in its leaves.

Lighting: The level of light should be reasonable—too high, and the leaves will fade or burn, but too low, and they will not open in the morning.

Watering: The prayer plant requires plenty of moisture. Keep the soil constantly moistened with warm water, but not soggy. Letting the soil go dry between waterings will harm the plant. Do not let the roots sit in the water.

Humidity: 50-60%. Enjoying a higher humidity level than most common households, using a humidifier might help.

Temperature: 65–70 °F.

Soil: Well-drained, loose soil with peat moss, sand, and loam works best for prayer plants.

Fertilizer: Feed sparingly during spring and summer with a water-soluble diluted fertilizer.

Propagation: These are easy to propagate by dividing the stems with roots attached during spring! Also, place cut stems and broken pieces in water and plant in soil once the roots are an inch long.

Toxicity: Non-poisonous.

71iStock.com/Arkela

Asparagaceae: Aspidistra elatior, "Cast Iron Plant"

This plant lives up to its name as a specimen that can live under challenging conditions. The leaves are dark green and oblong. It is essential to clean the leaves, removing dust and cobwebs to improve their photosynthesis ability.

The cast iron plant fits well in the living room, growing to 3 ft tall. It is a very slow grower and only requires occasional pruning of a yellow leaf plus a diluted dose of fertilizer during its growing months.

Lighting: It can thrive in shade or indirect light but must stay away from direct sunlight.

Watering: The cast iron plant can endure moisture in its planter, but a month without water in a 10-inch pot will not kill it. Water when the soil is nearly dry.

Humidity: This plant likes high humidity of about 50% but will do decently in lower humidity too.

Temperature: 64–75 °F.

Soil: Standard potting soil works.

Fertilizer: This plant does well without fertilizer but will appreciate a diluted hit every few months during spring and summer.

Propagation: Divide the root in spring, untangling the roots by hand and then dividing the rootstock into smaller pieces.

Toxicity: Nontoxic.

72iStock.com/Jamaludin Yusup

Commelinaceae: Tradescantia spathacea, "Oyster Plant"

This member of the Tradescantia genus is also called the Moses-in-the-cradle plant. Growing between 6 and 12 inches tall, the oyster plant has thin, green-and-purple-striped leaves that can grow to that same length. With its characteristic foliage, the oyster plant looks great the entire year with little maintenance, making it an excellent option for house-planting beginners and the desktop.

Lighting: These can keep in low light, but the ones grown under bright, indirect light will be more luxuriant.

Watering: The oyster plant is resistant to drought and only needs watering when the top inch of the soil feels dry to the touch. Do not overwater.

Humidity: 40% and above.

Temperature: 65–86 °F.

Soil: Rich but well-draining soil. These plants can die in heavy clay or silt-based soil, an issue identified if, after watering, the water does not soak into the soil readily. In this situation, removing the plant from the pot and replacing the soil with a better-aerated potting mix is best.

Fertilizer: This plant does not require intensive fertilizing. Feed it monthly during the growing season using a water-soluble diluted fertilizer.

Propagation: Divide side shoots from the main plant or root stem cuttings in water.

Toxicity: Nontoxic.

73iStock.com/lawcain

Polypodiaceae: Platycerium spp., "Staghorn Fern"

This plant is epiphytic, like air plants and orchids, meaning that it does not need soil to survive in nature and can just as easily attach to wood or moss. Pruning is not necessary.

Lighting: A staghorn fern likes bright, indirect light. It can tolerate a north-facing windowsill, but if the window is south-, east-, or west-facing, make sure it's a few feet away. This plant is prone to sun damage.

Watering: If the staghorn fern comes mounted on a wooden plank, treat it like an air plant: Mist it a couple of times a week and briefly submerge it if necessary. If it is in soil, keep it moist but not soggy—water once or twice a week, as necessary. It will dry out faster or slower, depending on the light levels.

Humidity: Very high, at 70%.

Temperature: 60–80 °F.

Soil: As mentioned, this plant can grow without soil. Attach it to a wooden plaque—use rot-resistant wood, such as cedar. To do this, wrap the fern with sphagnum moss and secure it with stretchy nylon bands made from used pantyhose, twine, or floral wire until its roots develop enough to anchor it. When opting for soil, ensure it is rich, coarse, and well-draining, with a high bark percentage and some peat content mixed in.

Fertilizer: Feed every 2 to 3 weeks during spring and summer.

Propagation: Dividing pups from the main plant is most efficient, but the spores can also make new staghorn ferns.

Toxicity: Nontoxic (Wolfe, 2021).

74iStock.com/QUAYSIDE

Asparagaceae: Dracaena sanderiana, "Lucky Bamboo"

The word "bamboo" is a misnomer; this plant is a member of the Dracaena family, along with corn plants and dragon trees. A low-maintenance plant that can grow to about 1–5 ft in height and 1–2 ft wide, the lucky bamboo is often offered as a gift and used to decorate homes and offices. A pruned corn (Lucky Bamboo) never regrows from that same top growth point again. Styled, it might have asymmetrical growth.

Lighting: Bright, filtered sunlight is best for lucky bamboo.

Watering: The lucky bamboo does not need much water, but please keep the soil damp. Soggy should not be the goal, but it can handle wetter conditions than other plants. This plant is sensitive to fluoride in tap water, so use conditioned, filtered or rainwater.

Humidity: 50% and upwards.

Temperature: 64–95 °F.

Soil: Cactus and succulent potting mixes are great.

Fertilizer: Feed once a month, if desired.

Propagation: Trim off cuttings from the plant and propagate them in water.

Toxicity: Toxic to animals and humans.

75iStock.com/scisettialfio

Pithophoraceae: Aegagropila linnaei, "Marimo Moss Balls"

These easy-to-care-for algae forms do well inside glass vases, bottles, or aquariums. In nature, they live at the bottom of cold lakes in Japan, which means they require little light to survive. The natural current tumbles the algae into a soft ball-like shape. As of the writing of this book, moss balls are not available in the U.S. due to a prohibition caused by environmental issues. They could become available in the future.

Lighting: This plant desires low light, but appreciates any indirect light given.

Watering: This is an aquatic plant, meaning it needs to stay submerged all the time. In place of watering, it needs airflow added to its environment and enough space to tumble gently.

Humidity: 100% (underwater). The tumbling movement keeps it healthy, and it is mesmerizing to watch.

Temperature: Below 77 °F. It will not live in hotter temperatures. Room temp should be fine.

Soil: It lives in water and does not use soil.

Fertilizer: None

Propagation: When a Marimo is huge, slice it into four more petite balls of at least an inch. Wrap each with twine, and they will develop into a ball shape.

Toxicity: Nontoxic.

76iStock.com/Sergey Melnichuk

Cactaceae: Rhipsalis salicornioides, "Dancing Bones Cactus"

With unique foliage and small yellow leaves, this cactus looks great in a planter. Its stems have the appearance of disjointed bones crossed together, forming a complex web that gives it a distinct look. Unlike most cacti, it works well in a hanging basket.

Lighting: This cactus can grow in the shade but prefers long hours of indirect light.

Watering: Only water when the soil is dry. Like any cactus, it is sensitive to watering before drying out.

Humidity: Low, 30–50%.

Temperature: 65–85 °F.

Soil: Cactus/succulent mix or well-draining sandy soil with perlite is best for this plant.

Fertilizer: Use fertilizer sparingly (every three months) at a quarter-diluted concentration.

Propagation: As with many cacti, this one propagates easily through cuttings placed on damp sandy soil.

Toxicity: Toxic to humans and animals.

77iStock.com/Dewin ˙ Indew

Alismataceae: Syngonium podophyllum, "Arrowhead Plant"

Nicknamed for its unique foliage, the arrowhead plant evolves from a pink arrow shape in young plants to split-lobe mature green leaves. It is a low-maintenance plant that thrives better indoors than outdoors.

Lighting: The plant adapts to low light and is a fast grower.

Watering: Keep the soil consistently moist. Arrowhead plants need watering when the top inch of the soil dries and do not like to dry out. However, they are still susceptible to root rot, so plan for good drainage.

Humidity: at least 40%.

Temperature: 60–80 °F.

Soil: Use rich potting soil with added compost.

Fertilizer: Fertilize once a month in warm seasons with a weak/diluted solution.

Propagation: Root stem cuttings in water or divide the plant at repotting.

Toxicity: Poisonous to humans and animals.

78iStock.com/Akchamczuk

Acanthaceae: Fittonia verschaffeltii, "Nerve Plant"

The nerve plant—whose name comes from the pink and white patterns on its leaves resembling human nerves—is a good companion plant for arrowheads, detailed in the previous entry. It does not need a large pot to grow, because its roots are shallow. Due to its easy-care requirements, it is excellent for beginners.

Lighting: Nerve plant prefers shade or indirect light, as it sunburns easily in higher light.

Watering: Keep the soil consistently moist; nerve plants do not like to dry out. However, they are still susceptible to root rot, so allow for good drainage.

Humidity: 50–70%. Responds well to misting and performs well in terrariums.

Temperature: 65–75 °F.

Soil: Average potting soil works.

Fertilizer: Use general fertilizer once or twice a year.

Propagation: Small cuttings placed in water will take 2–3 weeks to root.

Toxicity: Poisonous to humans and animals.

All of these plants will grow in low-light conditions but can benefit from some light. Each house is different, so explore each location and find the best spots where plants can grow. Always pay attention to the leaves: they tell you whether or not the plant is getting proper light. Add artificial light to your indoor garden and observe the differences if necessary. A cleverly-placed mirror can reflect more light into a room.

In the next chapter, we are going to see light-hungry plants. How much more energized do we feel after feeling the sun on our faces? For a plant, that's even more important since they need that light to produce food. Let's look at these divas and learn how to take good care of them.

79istock.com/kynny

CHAPTER 9:
SUN WORSHIPERS

BRIGHT LIGHT DIVAS

If a flowering plant whose movement is limited by its roots entrenched in the soil can choose to grow towards the light, why would you, with the freedom of limbs, choose darkness? –Quotes Empire

When we talk about intense light, the first thing that comes to mind is sunlight. It is, after all, the primary source of light available in nature. In this chapter, we will discuss plants that can only develop with plenty of light and how you can help them thrive. We'll see how to deal with them during summertime, when you might want to put them outdoors to enjoy the brightness, and what to do during colder seasons when the sunlight isn't as intense.

80istock.com/istock.com/kynny

Cycadaceae: Cycas revoluta, "Sago Palm"
The history of this plant goes back to the time before the dinosaurs. The shape of the sago palm leaves has granted it its popular name, even though it's not a genuine palm.

It is a slow grower and only produces one annual leaf on average. A sago palm will be 2–3 feet tall as a houseplant but may reach up to 10 feet outdoors. Getting to this size may take decades. Be careful when handling the sago's leaves: They are fragile, and if you bend one, the plant's recovery will be as slow as its growth.

Lighting: Sago palms require bright, indirect light for 6 to 8 hours per day.

Watering: They are sensitive to overwatering. The sago's trunk stores water and must be watered only when the soil gets dry.

Humidity: High, 50–75%.

Temperature: 65–75 °F.

Soil: Well-draining potting mix, cactus soil, or a combination of the two.

Fertilizer: Between April and October, feed once a month with a diluted liquid fertilizer.

Propagation: Divide pups from the parent plant; propagation by seed is slow.

Toxicity: Toxic to humans and animals (Vanzile, 2023).

8IiStock.com/nickkurzenko

Cyperaceae: Cyperus alternifolius, "Umbrella Papyrus" or "Umbrella Grass"

This pond plant is sometimes known as umbrella grass because of the appearance of its long stems and leaflets. Papyrus is very beginner friendly. It grows fast and is easy to care for and propagate as long as you remember, it lives in ponds in its natural habitat.

Lighting: The papyrus requires little maintenance. It loves 6 to 8 hours of bright light the most. It will not develop appropriately in the shade, however.

Watering: Papyrus is an aquatic plant indicating that it can tolerate waterlogging. Keep the roots of the umbrella papyrus damp. It is nearly impossible to kill through overwatering.

Humidity: At least 50%. Appreciates misting.

Temperature: 50–72 °F.

Soil: Papyrus needs moisture-retaining soil or potting soil mixed with ample peat moss.

Fertilizer: Fertilizer is not necessary, though you can give it monthly doses of a diluted fish emulsion solution.

Propagation: Divide roots and repot or root stem cuttings in water.

Toxicity: Toxic to humans and animals.

82iStock.com/dianazh

Oleaceae: Jasminum spp., "Jasmine"

Despite being a vine plant, jasmine can be grown indoors, where its heady scent is appreciated. The poet's jasmine (Jasminum grandiflorum) is the most common type of jasmine, whose petite white flowers last all summer. Jasminum officinale, or sweet jasmine, is another common variety. The vines climb through trellises and up poles, but you can prune them to keep them from taking control of your room.

Lighting: Jasmine requires bright, indirect light for 6 to 8 hours a day in order to bloom.

Watering: Do not let the planter pot go dry, as moist is preferred. Allow the soil to dry by a quarter between waterings. Water less in the cool season.

Humidity: 40–50%.

Temperature: 60°–75°F.

Soil: Regular potting soil, as long as it's well-draining works great; incorporate perlite or vermiculite for better drainage.

Fertilizer: Fertilize every 4–6 weeks during the growing period.

Propagation: Propagate from stem cuttings rooted in water.

Toxicity: Nontoxic (Jasmine, 2022).

83iStock.com/grafvision

Euphorbiaceae: Codiaeum variegatum, "Croton"

With its exuberant leaves displaying a range of various colors, this plant will make a bright statement in your home. Crotons come in many different varieties, identified by the shape and color of their leaves, which can go from resplendent yellow and white to more exotic colors, such as red, purple, orange, and pink.

Don't move your croton from outdoors to indoors or vice versa in seasons other than spring or fall, when the difference between indoors and outdoors is minimal. Try to keep it in the same light. Sudden changes will cause the leaves to drop off. Do wipe its leaves to get rid of dust and cobwebs.

Lighting: Bright, indirect light for the majority of the day benefits this plant.

Watering: Let it dry out between waterings. Retained moisture can cause its leaves to rot.

Humidity: High, 40–80%. In dry climates, mist or humidity will keep the plant's leaves from wilting.

Temperature: 55–80 °F.

Soil: It requires well-drained soil.

Fertilizer: Several types of fertilizer can work for crotons, preferably ones with lots of nitrogen and potassium. Feed every 2–3 months during spring and summer.

Propagation: Take a 3–4-inch stem cutting with at least three leaves and push it into moist soil at 70–80 °F temperature. Repot after a month.

Toxicity: Poisonous to humans and animals (Croton plant care, n.d.).

84iStock.com/Tatiana Terekhina

Crassulaceae: Echeveria elegans, "Mexican Snowball Succulent"

A healthy Echeveria plant, one of the most photogenic succulents, will bloom with pink flowers in spikes.

Lighting: Its beautiful rosette leaves require full sunlight to keep their shape. Rotate the plant to ensure that all sides receive equal light, or the plant will stretch, deforming the contours of its leaves.

Watering: The Echeveria requires little water, though thoroughly drench the plant when the soil completely dries. Be careful not to spray the leaves when watering or allow puddles of water to form inside the rosette, which will lead to rotting.

Humidity: 30–50%.

Temperature: 55–80 °F.

Soil: Well-draining soil, ideally cactus mix or potting soil with perlite and sand, is best.

Fertilizer: No fertilizing is required.

Propagation: Break off a leaf and allow it a couple of days to callus over before planting it shallowly, cut-side down, into the soil.

Toxicity: Nontoxic.

85iStock.com/seven75

Bignoniaceae: Radermachera sinica, "China Doll Plant"

The China doll plant has gained popularity as a houseplant due to its fern-like foliage. It has appealing, glossy leaflets, which make it look like a small tree. It is compact, maintains a graceful and elegant appearance, and is easy to find in nurseries.

The China doll plant must be kept from drafts, as it is sensitive to environmental changes. Even when the weather outdoors shifts through the seasons, you have to keep the indoor conditions consistent, or the plant will feel it and respond.

Lighting: China doll plants need bright, indirect light for hours on end.

Watering: The plant should be allowed to dry out slightly between waterings, but it needs regular and consistent watering.

Humidity: 40% or higher.

Temperature: 65–75 °F.

Soil: Use a well-draining but rich potting mix.

Fertilizer: Liquid houseplant fertilizer every few months is sufficient.

Propagation: Remove a 2– to 3-inch green-wood cutting from the plant and place it in the soil. Cover with a plastic bag or clear container, and place in a warm area. The plastic bag or cover will keep the humidity from escaping and create the climatic conditions for the cutting to root, which should take a few weeks.

Toxicity: Non-Toxic.

86iStock.com/CataFratto

Lamiaceae: Ocimum basilicum, "Basil"

This tropical herb is a culinary favorite in diverse cuisines and cultures. It can be finicky for beginners to keep alive, though it is worth it for those who enjoy cooking (or its fragrant scent). If you have to trim the plant, that shouldn't be a problem—the trimmings are edible and delicious! This plant is an excellent introduction to growing fresh herbs. Basil will flower indoors with a spike of tiny white, pink, or purple blooms.

Lighting: Long hours of bright, indirect light is best for basil. It wilts and scorches easily in direct sunlight and grows pale and lanky in shaded areas.

Watering: Only water once or twice a week. Basil does not like to be too damp or dry; it is highly sensitive to both. It should be kept as consistently moist (but not wet) as possible.

Humidity: 40–60%. Keep it draft-free.

Temperature: 55–80 °F.

Soil: Use rich but well-draining potting mix or vegetable soil, preferably organic.

Fertilizer: Fertilize with an organic fertilizer every 4–6 weeks. It will not be guaranteed safe to eat if it is not organic.

Propagation: Remove a 2–3-inch green-wood cutting from the plant and root it in water. Change the water every other day, or it will rot. You can also try rooting cuttings in soil by placing them in potting mix, covering them with a plastic bag, and putting that somewhere warm.

Toxicity: Non-Toxic.

87iStock.com/satura86

Asparagaceae: Dracaena marginata, "Dragon Tree"

The dragon tree is a low-maintenance indoor plant with a strong trunk and thin leaves, making your home more attractive while purifying your air. It will grow slowly but steadily. Choose a big deep container for this Dracaena to give its extensive root system space to develop and grow. The old leaves of the dragon plant will drop as the new ones take their place.

Lighting: Dragon tree needs 6-8 hours of bright, indirect light.

Watering: Water as a succulent by drenching the soil thoroughly and letting it drain, then dry completely; this is a tolerant plant, but the tips of leaves can go brown if you give it too much water. It is sensitive to minerals, so use conditioned water, rainwater, or fish tank water.

Humidity: 50% and upwards.

Temperature: 70–80 °F.

Soil: Try a well-drained standard potting soil with peat moss.

Fertilizer: During the growing season (spring through fall), apply a balanced fertilizer every 2 weeks.

Propagation: Stem cuttings in water or soil, or propagation by air-layering, begin to sprout roots in about 3 weeks.

Toxicity: Toxic to humans and animals.

88iStock.com/soniabonet

Asteraceae: Senecio rowleyanus, "String of Pearls"

This succulent has a unique appearance, with orb-shaped water-storing leaves that inspired its popular name. These grow on trailing vines that resemble necklaces and can grow several feet long.

Placing the string of pearls in a pot that's too large will keep the soil wet, causing the leaves in direct contact with the soil to rot. There are many varieties of string plants; banana, dolphin, heart, etc., and they are stunning and fun to collect.

Lighting: Some exposure to bright, direct light is ideal, but consistent indirect light works too.

Watering: Usually watering only once or twice a month is needed. Once watered thoroughly, allow the soil to dry out. The pearls will dimple if the plant needs more water. The plant cannot recover from too much water. Decrease watering during winter.

Humidity: 30–50%.

Temperature: 60–90 °F.

Soil: It likes well-draining soil that goes dry, like a cactus potting mix or ⅔ regular potting soil mixed with ⅓ coarse sand.

Fertilizer: Fertilize once a month, if desired. No fertilizer in fall or winter, please. Dilute the fertilizer and apply it after watering so it doesn't overwhelm the plant. Overfertilizing could kill your string of pearls, as with many other succulents.

Propagation: Lay a cutting 3–4 inches long on the soil and pin the cuttings to the top of the potting mixture; roots will gradually emerge. Another option is to remove the bottom few pearls so they do not rot and then place the stem cuttings in water.

Toxicity: Toxic to humans and animals.

89iStock.com/bruev

Acanthaceae: Haworthiopsis Fasciata, "Zebra Plant"

The zebra plant looks like an aloe vera, apart from the stripes to which it owes its name. Unlike aloe vera, it's not poisonous to cats and dogs and generates white or pink flowers on top of a tall, thin stem. The zebra plant grows in groups, with tubercles or nodules under the surface, and is ideal for beginners due to its low care requirements. It doesn't mind neglect.

Lighting: The zebra plant requires plenty of bright light, at least 4–6 hours daily.

Watering: Like any succulent or cactus, it requires a drench, drain, and dry watering routine. Water the planter thoroughly. Allow all the water to drain out and then remove any leftover drips from the cache pot. Do not water again until after the planter has gone dry.

Humidity: 30–50%.

Temperature: 64–75 °F.

Soil: Use a cactus/succulent mix or a 3-to-1 ratio of coarse sand to potting soil.

Fertilizer: Every month during the spring and early summer, you can apply a water-soluble commercial fertilizer designed for cacti or use quarter-strength dilution.

Propagation: These plants multiply profusely through offshoot propagation. Gently dump the plant out of its pot, then shake and pull the plants apart. Let them dry off in a cool place for a few days before repotting in the proper mixture.

Toxicity: Nontoxic.

CALL TO ACTION
REVIEW PAGE

I'd love to hear your feedback about this book. I created it as a guide and friend to consult whenever you need advice. If you want to share your journey about growing indoor plants and help me to reach more readers, consider leaving a quick Amazon review. You will be helping me to get more visibility and also helping other people who are thinking about starting this hobby and need help knowing where to begin.

CONCLUSION

There's a reason why some people like to bring plastic plants to their houses. Fake plants don't need care; they don't get sick, they're easy to clean, and you can get rid of them without remorse. Between that and growing a living plant indoors, there's an ocean of differences.

Plants aren't differentiated only by their looks. Each of them has distinct needs and characteristics. Many enjoy similar conditions and care. I hope that, from all the plants we've discussed in this book, you have been able to pick the ones that will fit well in your home with your lifestyle. Some of these plants are fussier than others and will require more attention, but it pays off when you see them growing and filling your home with life.

As we end, I hope you feel more confident about committing to a houseplant journey. The information on plant physiology, common sense solutions (if this then that), and indoor gardening methods serves to impart a way of understanding plant care that will decrease anxiety and make you more successful rearing houseplants of all kinds. Remember to check growing requirements to choose the best plant for the location you have in mind. Be mindful of keeping children and pets safe from toxic plants.

Once a plant gets the understanding, care, and love it needs, chances are it will live for years to come. It will become a part of your house and your family as you watch it go through the different stages of its lifespan. Be there for your plant at its worst, and it will reward you with its best.

I can't imagine my life without plants, and that awareness drove me to write this book you've just read.

Now it's your turn. Walk around your home and select places where you will fit your tropical houseplants. Don't stop there! Share your plants with your friends and family, and encourage them to raise houseplants!

REFERENCES

5 fascinating things you didn't know about cacti. (2020, July 18). *Apartment Therapy.* https://www.apartmenttherapy.com/cactus-plants-265228

6 steps to keep African violets blooming. (2021, January 20). *Espoma Organic.* https://www.espoma.com/flowers/6-steps-to-keep-african-violets-blooming/

7 best planter materials: Expert guide to help you choose your next planter. (2021, May 19). *Jay Scotts Collection.* https://jayscotts.com/blog/planter-materials

The 8 best plant moisture meters for 2023. (2023, January 19). *The Spruce.* https://www.thespruce.com/best-moisture-meters-for-plants-4801862

12 different types of bromeliad plants. (n.d.). *Amaze Vege Garden.* https://www.amazevegegarden.com/different-types-of-bromeliad-plants/

20 types of begonias: Flowers, leaves (with pictures, identification, and care guide). (n.d.). *Leafy Place.* https://leafyplace.com/begonia-types/

A detailed guide for indoor cyclamen! (n.d.). *UK Houseplants.* https://www.ukhouseplants.com/plants/cyclamen

African Violets. (n.d.). *Almanac.com.* https://www.almanac.com/plant/african-violets

Akin, C. (2022, February 19). The beginner's guide to cast iron plant care. *Houseplant Resource Center.* https://houseplantresourcecenter.com/2021/03/the-beginners-guide-to-cast-iron-plant-care/

Allen Smith, P. Stop your corn plant from turning brown on the tips. (2020, January 24). *P. Allen Smith.* https://pallensmith.com/2015/12/14/corn-plant-turning-brown-on-the-tips/

All families — The plant list. (n.d.). http://www.theplantlist.org/browse/-/

Andrychowicz, A. (2022, November 6). How to care for a lipstick plant (Aeschynanthus radicans). *Get Busy Gardening.* https://getbusygardening.com/lipstick-plant-care/

Antosh, G. (2023, January 3). Is the popular succulent jade plant poisonous or toxic? *Plant Care Today.* https://plantcaretoday.com/jade-plant-poisonous.html

Antosh, G. (2023a, February 21). Fertilizing croton plants: When and how to fertilize crotons. *Plant Care Today.* https://plantcaretoday.com/croton-fertilizer.html

Antosh, G. (2023b, February 27). Growing Hatiora salicornioides: Caring for dancing bones cactus. *Plant Care Today.* https://plantcaretoday.com/hatiora-salicornioides.html

Antosh, G. (n.d.). Natal mahogany. *Plant Care.* http://www.plant-care.com/natal-mahogany-house-plant-for-overwaterers.html

Araceae (Colocasia/Taro) - Care tips. (2022, November 4). *PLNTS.com.* https://plnts.com/en/care/houseplants-family/araceae

Arrowhead plant care. (2021, October 29). *Bloomscape.* https://bloomscape.com/plant-care-guide/arrowhead-plant/

Asparagaceae: BoDD. (n.d.). https://www.botanical-dermatology-database.info/BotDermFolder/ASPA.html

Asparagus fern care. (2021, December 13). *Bloomscape.* https://bloomscape.com/plant-care-guide/asparagus-fern/

Blaky. (2021, June 9). 15 different types of ficus plants for home and garden. *Go Get Yourself.* https://www.gogetyourself.com/15-different-types-of-ficus-plants-for-home-and-garden/

Baessler, L. (n.d.). Schefflera plant pruning: Tips on cutting back Schefflera plants. *Gardening Know How.* https://www.gardeningknowhow.com/houseplants/schefflera/schefflera-plant-pruning.htm.

Baron, K. (2022a, September 24). Everything you need to know about indoor anthurium care. *HappySprout.* https://www.happysprout.com/indoor-plants/anthurium-care/

Baron, K. (2022b, November 10). How do you care for a peace lily indoors? It's easier than you think. *HappySprout.* https://www.happysprout.com/indoor-plants/how-do-you-care-for-a-peace-lily-indoors/

Baron, K. (2022c, December 26). Don't know how often you need to water your cactus? We have answers that might surprise you. *HappySprout.* https://www.happysprout.com/indoor-plants/how-often-to-water-cactus/

Bawden-Davis, J. (2021, March 31). Polka dot plant care! How to grow pink polka dot plants indoors. *Parade.com.* https://parade.com/845822/juliebawdendavis/grow-polka-dot-plant-in-your-indoor-garden/

Bird of paradise care. (2019, October 17.). *Greenery: Unlimited.* https://greeneryunlimited.co/blogs/plant-care/bird-of-paradise-care

Blackstone, V. L. (2018, December 17). What advantages does the waxy cuticle provide to the leaf? *SFGate.* https://homeguides.sfgate.com/advantages-waxy-cuticle-provide-leaf-92502.html

Brown, S. (2023, February 3). 17 natural and homemade pesticides for plants. *Dre Campbell Farm.* https://drecampbell.com/natural-homemade-insecticides/

C., K. (2022a, November 2). Ficus triangularis plant care. *Plantly.* https://plantly.io/plant-care/ficus-triangularis/

C., K. (2022b, March 11). 22 houseplant combination ideas. *Balcony Garden Web.* https://balconygardenweb.com/houseplant-combination-ideas/

Carroll, J. (2022, October 19). Growing areca palm: Care of areca palms indoors. *Gardening Know How.* https://www.gardeningknowhow.com/houseplants/areca-palm/growing-areca-palm-indoors.htm

Castelaz, C. (2019, January 28). 10 huge houseplants that make a statement. *Bob Vila.* https://www.bobvila.com/slideshow/10-huge-houseplants-that-make-a-statement-52621

Chang, R. (2022, June 10). The 8 best indoor plants for the office, according to plant experts. *Buy Side From WSJ.* https://www.wsj.com/buyside/home/best-plants-for-office-01653412461

Churchill, A. (2015, May 8). Eight tips for safely transporting your houseplants during a move. *Martha Stewart.* https://www.marthastewart.com/1113965/moving-tips-transporting-houseplants

Combiths, S. (2022a, September 8). The heartleaf philodendron is harder to kill than to keep alive. *Apartment Therapy.* https://www.apartmenttherapy.com/philodendron-plant-heartleaf-care-growing-toxicity-256104

Combiths, S. (2022b, September 13). How to care for and maintain your unique prayer plants. *Apartment Therapy.* https://www.apartmenttherapy.com/prayer-plants-maranta-care-258069

Common houseplant diseases: Identification and treatment. (2020, March 8). *Smart Garden Guide.* https://smartgardenguide.com/common-houseplant-diseases/

Connor, C. (2022, December 5). Best indoor plants for beginners. *The Greenhouse Blog by Plants.com.* https://www.plants.com/greenhouse/plant-care/plants-for-beginners/

Contributor. (2020, September 8). How to care for a Meyer lemon tree indoors. *SF Gate.* https://homeguides.sfgate.com/care-meyer-lemon-tree-indoors-56494.html

Coulter, L. (2020, October 30). 21 indoor plants for low light. HGTV. https://www.hgtv.com/outdoors/flowers-and-plants/houseplants/14-indoor-plants-for-low-light-pictures.

Croton plant care: An ultimate guide. (n.d.). *Ambius.* https://www.ambius.com/learn/plant-doctor/ultimate-guides/ultimate-guide-croton-plant-care/

Daniel. (2021, February 24). Peace lily plant care guide: Killer tips you wish you knew earlier. *Plantophiles.* https://plantophiles.com/plant-care/peace-lily/

Diffusion in plants. (2021, February 8). *BYJUS.* https://byjus.com/biology/diffusion-means-of-transport/

Does talking to plants really make them grow? (2022, February 18). *The Spruce.* https://www.thespruce.com/should-you-talk-to-your-plants-3972298

Dracaena care. (n.d.). Mashrita Nature Cloud. https://www.mashrita.com/dracaena-care-asparagaceae-care

Dyer, M. H. (2022, September 19). What is copper fungicide – How to use copper fungicide in gardens. *Gardening Know How.* https://www.gardeningknowhow.com/garden-how-to/info/what-is-copper-fungicide.htm

English ivy plant care. (n.d.). https://www.guide-to-houseplants.com/english-ivy.html

Euphorbia ammak . "African candelabra." (2020, November 5). *Succulents Network.* https://succulentsnetwork.com/euphorbia-ammak-africancandelabra-care-guide

Falkenthal, G. L. (2022a, December 28). How long do plants live? *Good Earth Plants.* https://www.goodearthplants.com/how-long-do-plants-live/

Flowers Quotes II. (n.d.). http://www.notable-quotes.com/f/flowers_quotes_ii.html

Foster, N. (2022, June 23). Buying houseplants: 14 tips for indoor gardening newbies. *Joy Us Garden.* https://www.joyusgarden.com/how-to-buy-houseplants/

Francis, M. (n.d.). How to grow a ficus tree indoors. *HGTV.* https://www.hgtv.com/outdoors/flowers-and-plants/houseplants/how-to-grow-a-ficus-tree-indoors

Fresh, F. (2021, June 12). 15 common indoor plant problems: Treatment, prevention and care tips. *FTD.com.* https://www.ftd.com/blog/share/plant-problems

Friendship plant care tips - Pilea involucrata "Moon Valley." (n.d.). *Guide to Houseplants.* https://www.guide-to-houseplants.com/friendship-plant.html

George, L. (2023, February 9). How to care for and grow your dragon tree. *La Résidence.* https://blog.leonandgeorge.com/posts/how-to-care-and-grow-dragon-tree-dracaena

Glossary of houseplant terminology. (n.d.). https://howmanyplants.com/post/glossary-of-houseplant-terminology

Goldfish plant care tips: How to grow Columnea gloriosa indoors. (n.d.). https://www.guide-to-houseplants.com/goldfish-plant.html

Grant, B. L. (2021, June 14). Ponytail palm propagation: Propagating ponytail palm pups. *Gardening Know How.* https://www.gardeningknowhow.com/houseplants/ponytail-palm/propagating-ponytail-palm-pups.htm

Grant, B. L. (2021, June 23). Euphorbia plant care. *Gardening Know How.* https://www.gardeningknowhow.com/ornamental/cacti-succulents/euphorbia/growing-euphorbia-plants.htm

Green, D. (n.d.). Begonia maculata care – How to grow an indoor polka dot begonia. *Mod And Mint Plant Care.* https://www.modandmint.com/polkadot-begonia-maculata-plant-care/

Grow towards the light and move out of the darkness. (2018, March 1). *Quotes Empire.* https://quotesempire.com/motivational-quotes/grow-towards-the-light/

Hassani, N. (2021, April 12). How to grow satin pothos (Scindapsus pictus). *The Spruce.* https://www.thespruce.com/growing-satin-pothos-5114102

Home. (n.d.). *The Plant List.* http://www.theplantlist.org/1/

Home. (n.d.). *World Flora Online.* http://www.worldfloraonline.org/

Horton, R. P. (2021, June 11). What are air plants and how do they grow? *Family Handyman.* https://www.familyhandyman.com/article/grow-air-plants/

Hossain, M. D. (2022, August 29). Mystery solved: How big do ponytail palms grow? *Club Gardening.* https://clubgardening.com/ponytail-palm-how-big-do-they-grow/

How long do African violets live? (2022, April 2). *Plant Index.* https://www.plantindex.com/african-violets-lifespan/

How to care for a Peperomia obtusifolia or baby rubber plant. (2022, January 14). *The Sill.* https://www.thesill.com/blog/how-to-care-for-baby-rubber-plant-peperomia-obtusifolia

How to care for a ZZ plant or Zamioculcas zamiifolia. (2022, June 7). *The Sill* https://www.thesill.com/blog/how-to-care-for-zz-zamioculcas-zamiifolia

How to care for an areca palm. (2021, May 2). *Plant Care for Beginners.* https://plantcareforbeginners.com/articles/how-to-care-for-an-areca-palm

How to care for string of pearls plant. (n.d.). *Succulents Box.* https://succulentsbox.com/blogs/blog/how-to-care-for-string-of-pearls

How to choose the best indoor plant for you. (n.d.). *Bloomscape.* https://bloomscape.com/green-living/how-to-choose-the-best-indoor-plant-for-you/

How to grow and care for a Meyer lemon tree. (2022, December 28). *Architectural Digest.* https://www.architecturaldigest.com/reviews/home-products/meyer-lemon-tree#:~:

How to grow basil indoors. (n.d.). *Gardener's Supply.* https://www.gardeners.com/how-to/basil-indoors/8930.html

How to grow kentia palm (Howea forsteriana). (2021, July 28). *BBC Gardeners' World Magazine.* https://www.gardenersworld.com/how-to/grow-plants/how-to-grow-kentia-palm-howea-forsteriana/

How to grow indoor cyclamen. (2022, September 8). *BBC Gardeners' World Magazine.* https://www.gardenersworld.com/how-to/grow-plants/how-to-grow-indoor-cyclamen/

How to grow Phalaenopsis (moth orchids). (n.d.). *Royal Horticultural Society.* https://www.rhs.org.uk/plants/phalaenopsis/growing-guide

How to grow satin pothos (Scindapsus pictus). (2021, April 12). *The Spruce.* https://www.thespruce.com/growing-satin-pothos-5114102

How to grow succulents. (2023, February 21). *BBC Gardeners' World Magazine.* https://www.gardenersworld.com/how-to/grow-plants/how-to-grow-succulents/

How to properly water indoor plants. (2018, November 22). *Millcreek Gardens.* https://www.millcreekgardens.com/how-to-properly-water-indoor-plants/

How to repot your houseplant. (2022, May 18). The Sill. (https://www.thesill.com/blog/plant-care-repotting

How to spot 6 common houseplant pests and safely kill them. (2023, January 31). *Better Homes & Gardens.* https://www.bhg.com/gardening/houseplants/care/common-houseplant-pests/

How to take care of a Hoya. (2022, April 8). *Plant Care for Beginners.* https://plantcareforbeginners.com/articles/how-to-take-care-of-a-hoya

How to take care of Norfolk Island pines. (n.d.). https://www.pennington.com/all-products/fertilizer/resources/nurturing-norfolk-island-pines-year-round

Jasmine. (2022, May 4.). *Old Farmer's Almanac.* https://www.almanac.com/plant/jasmine

Johnson, N. (2022, April 27). 5 tips for picking healthy plants at the nursery. *Birds and Blooms.* https://www.birdsandblooms.com/gardening/gardening-basics/gardening-basics-5-tips-choosing-plants-nursery/

Jones, A. (2022, July 7). How to grow jade plant (lucky plant). *MyDomaine.* https://www.mydomaine.com/how-to-care-for-your-jade-plant-the-complete-guide-4693652

Joyner, L. (2020, July 17). 10 common houseplants that can be toxic if ingested. *House Beautiful.* https://www.housebeautiful.com/uk/garden/plants/g33306866/toxic-plants/

Judy. (2022, December 27). Natal mahogany plant. *Houseplant 411.* https://www.houseplant411.com/houseplant/natal-mahogany-plant-how-to-grow-care-guide/#

Kelly, T. (2022, August 5). Money tree propagation: Growing new plants from cuttings. *The Healthy Houseplant.* https://thehealthyhouseplant.com/money-tree-propagation-growing-new-plants-from-cuttings/

Kingdom Plantae. (n.d.). *First-Learn.com.* https://www.first-learn.com/kingdom-plantae.html

Lady palm. (n.d.). *Guide to Houseplants.* https://www.guide-to-houseplants.com/lady-palm.html

Larano, L. (2020, August 28). How to care for your jade plant. *Omysa.* https://omysa.com/blogs/planting-101/how-to-care-for-your-jade-plant#:~:text=Feed%20your%20Jade%20plant%20with,a%20fertilizer%20with%20less%20nitrogen.

LaVolpe, N. (2022, July 7). 8 tips to grow big, bushy basil. *Farmers' Almanac.* https://www.farmersalmanac.com/8-tips-to-grow-big-bushy-basil

Lee, M. (2015, April 28). Interaction with indoor plants may reduce psychological and physiological stress by suppressing autonomic nervous system activity in young adults: a randomized crossover study. *Journal of Physiological Anthropology.* BioMed Central. https://jphysiolanthropol.biomedcentral.com/articles/10.1186/s40101-015-0060-8

Lighting indoor houseplants. (n.d.). *MU Extension.* https://extension.missouri.edu/publications/g6515

Lloyster, M. (2022, September 12). Sago palm. *Houseplants Expert.* https://www.houseplantsexpert.com/sago-palm.html

Lucky bamboo care guide. (2021, August 3). *Proflowers Blog.* https://www.proflowers.com/blog/lucky-bamboo-care

Mahr, S. (n.d.). String of pearls, Senecio rowleyanus. *Wisconsin Horticulture.* https://hort.extension.wisc.edu/articles/string-of-pearls-senecio-rowleyanus/

Main ficus species and care for them. (n.d.). *Ficusplant.* https://ficusplant.org/types-of-ficuses/

Martin, K. (2022, July 22). 10 natural fertilizers for houseplants. *Urban Garden Gal.* https://www.urbangardengal.com/natural-fertilizers-houseplants/

Massura, C. (2022, October 15). How to propagate snake plant: 4 sure-fire methods (Steps + FAQs). *Rosy Soil.* https://rosysoil.com/blogs/news/how-to-propagate-snake-plant

McCarthy, A. (2023, January 22). 20 tips and tricks for new plant parents. *Yardbarker.* https://www.yardbarker.com/lifestyle/articles/20_tips_and_tricks_for_new_plant_parents/s1__35111042

McIntosh, J. (2022, June 30). 20 types of orchids to use as houseplants. *The Spruce.* https://www.thespruce.com/orchid-identification-1315976

Miller, C. (2022, November 21). How to care for devil's ivy. *Bustling Nest.* https://bustlingnest.com/how-to-care-for-devils-ivy/

Money tree 101: How to care for money trees. (n.d.). *Bloomscape.* https://bloomscape.com/plant-care-guide/money-tree/

Morrow, M. (2020, July 16). 9.3: *Leaf anatomy.* Biology LibreTexts. https://bio.libretexts.org/Bookshelves/Botany/Botany_Lab_Manual_(Morrow)/09:_Leaf_Anatomy/9.3:_Leaf_Anatomy

Natal mahogany care instructions. (n.d.). *Plantify Urban Plantery.* https://plantify.co.za/pages/natal-mahogany-care-instructions

Nerve plant care: How to grow Fittonia verschaffeltii indoors. (n.d.). *Guide To Houseplants.* https://www.guide-to-houseplants.com/nerve-plant.html

Neveln, V. (2023, January 23). How to care for China doll plant. *Better Homes & Gardens.* https://www.bhg. com/gardening/plant-dictionary/houseplant/china-doll/

Norfolk Island pines. (n.d.). *Penn State University.* https://extension.psu.edu/norfolk-island-pines

Oyster plant care (Tradescantia spathacea). (2020, November 27). *Smart Garden* Guide. https:// smartgardenguide.com/oyster-plant-care-tradescantia-spathacea/

A plant for every room: Choosing the right houseplant for each space. (2021, April 19). *Plants Spark Joy.* https:// www.plantssparkjoy.com/right-houseplant-for-each-room-space/

Perfect combination: Houseplants that can be planted together and pairings to avoid. (2022, September 5). *Plants Spark Joy.* https://www.plantssparkjoy.com/houseplants-that-can-be-planted-together/

Photosynthesis. (n.d.). *National Geographic.* https://education.nationalgeographic.org/resource/ photosynthesis/

Plant classification and how it works. (2023, February 14). *American Meadows.* https://www.americanmeadows. com/plant-classification

Plant kingdom. (2022, November 29). *VEDANTU.* https://www.vedantu.com/biology/plant-kingdom

Plant root. (n.d.). *StudySmarter US.* https://www.studysmarter.us/explanations/biology/plant-biology/plant-root/

Plant stem: Functions, parts and types. (2021, May 24). *SmartClass4Kids.* https://smartclass4kids.com/plant-stem/

Queen's tears: growing and caring for Queen's tears. (n.d.) *Garden Lovers Club.* https://www.gardenloversclub. com/houseplants/queens-tears/growing-queens-tears/

Ripley, B. S. (1999, July). Function of leaf hairs revisited: The hair layer on leaves Arctotheca populifolia reduces photoinhibition, but leads to higher leaf temperatures caused by lower transpiration rates. *Science Direct.* https://www.sciencedirect.com/science/article/abs/pii/S0176161799801436

Russell, E. M. (n.d.). Hydrogen peroxide for houseplants, fully explained. *Gardening Channel.* https://www. gardeningchannel.com/hydrogen-peroxide-for-houseplants-explained/

Sanders, G. (2022, March 9). Beginner's guide to the asparagus fern. *The Green Mad House.* https://www. thegreenmadhouse.com/plants/beginners-guide-to-the-asparagus-fern#:~:text=Asparagus%20 ferns%20also%20like%20a,will%20yellow%20and%20drop%20needles.

Sansevieria 101: How to care for snake plants. (n.d.). *Bloomscape.* https://bloomscape.com/plant-care-guide/ sansevieria/

Schillinger, L. (2023, March 16). How to divide potted plants & plant pups. *Bloombox Club.* https://bloomboxclub. com/blogs/news/how-to-divide-potted-plants-and-plant-pups

Shehata, S. (2021, September 2). Top tips to care for your oxalis triangularis. *Greenarium.* https://greenarium. uk/plants-a-z/plant-care-guide/humata-tyermannii-fern-rabbits-foot-fern-3rs5j-tft5m

Shinn, M. (2020, January 31). Echeveria plant care indoors. *Horticulture.* https://www.hortmag.com/plants-we-love-2/echeveria-plant-care-indoors

Should you mist tour houseplants? (2022, September 20). *Treehugger.* https://www.treehugger.com/when-mist-your-houseplants-4858667

Signs of disease in common houseplants. (n.d.). *Bioadvanced.* https://bioadvanced.com/signs-common-houseplant-diseases

Slik, J. W. F., Arroyo-Rodríguez, V., Aiba, S. I., Alvarez-Loayza, P., Alves, L. F., Ashton, P., Balvanera, P., Bastian, M. L., Bellingham, P. J., Van Den Berg, E., Bernacci, L., Da Conceição Bispo, P., Blanc, L., Böhning-Gaese, K., Boeckx, P., Bongers, F., Boyle, B., Bradford, M., Brearley, M., & Breuer-Doundou Hockemba, M. (2015). An estimate of the number of tropical tree species. *Proceedings of the National Academy of Sciences, 112(24),* 7472–7477. https://pnas.org/doi/full/10.1073/pnas.1423147112

Slim, J. (2022, October 6). How to easily root and propagate a cactus step-by-step. *Succulent Plant Care.* https://succulentplantcare.com/how-to-easily-root-and-propagate-a-cactus/

Snake plant. (n.d.). *Leaf Envy.* https://www.leafenvy.co.uk/blogs/plant-a-z/snake-plant

Thorne, E. (2022, September 1). Our complete guide to fiddle leaf fig care. *Stump Curated Plants.* https://stumpplants.com/journal/fiddle-leaf-fig-guide

Tom. (n.d.). Umbrella grass (Cyperus alternifolius / Papyrus). *Our House Plants.* https://www.ourhouseplants.com/plants/umbrella-grass-cyperus

Turner, C. (2022, October 11). 10 poisonous indoor plants your children and pets should avoid. *My Tasteful Space.* https://blog.mytastefulspace.com/2020/03/04/poisonous-indoor-plants/

Tuttle, C. (2022, October 4). Haworthiopsis fasciata "zebra plant." *Succulents and Sunshine.* https://www.succulentsandsunshine.com/types-of-succulents/haworthia-fasciata-zebra-plant/

Vanzile, J. (2022, January 23). How to grow and care for sago palm. *The Spruce.* https://www.thespruce.com/grow-sago-palms-1902770

Vanzile, J. (2023a, March 14). Philodendron varieties: How to grow indoors. *The Spruce.* https://www.thespruce.com/grow-philodendron-houseplants-1902768

Vanzile, J. (2023b, March 11). Learn how to grow and care for yucca plant indoors. *The Spruce.* https://www.thespruce.com/grow-yucca-inside-1902500

Vernoux, T. (2010, March 24). Auxin at the shoot apical meristem. *National Library of Medicine.* https://pubmed.ncbi.nlm.nih.gov/20452945/

Walliser, J. (2022, December 3). Houseplant fertilizer basics: How and when to feed houseplants. *Savvy Gardening.* https://savvygardening.com/houseplant-fertilizer/

Weir, K. (2020, April 1). Nurtured by nature. *American Psychological Association.* https://www.apa.org/monitor/2020/04/nurtured-nature

What are the parts of a plant and flower? (Gardening basics). (2022, October 3). *Planet Natural.* https://www.planetnatural.com/plant-anatomy/Williams, D. (2023, January 23). Baby tears plant care guide. *The Contented Plant.* https://thecontentedplant.com/baby-tears-plant-care-guide/

Winter Care: Caring For Plants. (n.d.). *Bioadvanced.* https://bioadvanced.com/winter-care-house-plants

Wolfe, M. (2021, August 23). Staghorn fern care: Mastering this exotic, easy-to-grow conversation piece. *Bob Vila.* https://www.bobvila.com/articles/staghorn-fern-care/

Women's voices are found to make plants grow faster. (2009, June 23). *N.P.R.* https://www.npr.org/templates/story/story.php?storyId=105797372

Wooden planters are good for your plant's health! (n.d*.). Plantscapes.* https://plantscapes.ae/wooden-planters-are-good-for-your-plants-health/

YR9 Topic 5: Plant structure and photosynthesis. (n.d.). *Amazing World of Science with Mr. Green.* https://www.mrgscience.com/yr9-topic-5-plant-structure-and-photosynthesis.html

Images

Alan 4 U TW. (2022, October 5). Bathroom plants. Https://Pixabay.com/Photos/Plant-Tub-Bathroom-Hygiene-7498330/.

Lubos. (2018, April 30). Pretty orange flowers. Pixabay.

Wdadiya, F. (2020, September 17). Indoor courtyard full of plants. Pixabay. https://pixabay.com/photos/building-plants-pots-decoration-5572186/

Cover Design

Nanne-99Designs.

Made in the USA
Las Vegas, NV
12 September 2024

95143461R00085